The Doctrine of Scripture

The Doctrine of Scripture

Locus 2 of
Institutio theologiae elencticae

Francis Turretin

Edited and Translated by
John W. Beardslee III

BAKER BOOK HOUSE
Grand Rapids, Michigan 49506

ISBN: Cloth: 0-8010-8858-5
       Paper: 0-8010-8857-7

Printed in the United States of America

Contents

74304

Contents

Introduction

Years ago, when the translation and publication of some works by Reformed scholastics was proposed, a leading American church historian spoke in opposition, declaring that nobody wanted to read that stuff. Experience with my *Reformed Dogmatics*,[1] and in the classroom, suggests that he was not altogether wrong, but there are today signs of interest in the field. And whether the interest be great or small, there are good reasons for making more of the scholastic orthodoxy of Protestantism available for English readers. James R. Willson wrote in 1817: "The doctrines of the Genevan school will bear the severest examination when brought to the Law and the Testimony. They have been blessed by God for the promotion of personal piety and will yet be blessed for that end."[2] In emphasizing both

1. John W. Beardslee III, ed. and trans., *Reformed Dogmatics: J. Wollebius, G. Voetius, F. Turretin* (New York: Oxford University Press, 1965; reprint ed., Grand Rapids: Baker, 1977).

2. James R. Willson, *A Historical Sketch of Opinions on the Atonement . . . with Translations from Francis Turretin* (Philadelphia: Edward Earle, 1817), p. viii.

7

God's use of human means and the development of personal piety, he was on Francis Turretin's own ground, even as, in offering a translation of a section of Turretin's work as an antidote for deviations from strict orthodoxy, he was also following this Genevan. The subsequent use of Turretin's theology in the United States, especially in the Princeton theology that culminated in the work of Charles Hodge, affords vivid proof of the fact that, two centuries after it had been written, it was still viable as an intellectual and practical expression of Christianity. It was so viable because it could serve the interests of practical piety, and because it was conceived and organized in a way that met the demands of a disciplined mind.

To understand his lasting contributions, a few words should be said, first about Francis Turretin, and then about Reformed scholastic orthodoxy and its doctrine of Scripture.

Francis Turretin (to use the form in which the name Turrettini was most commonly written by the older American theologians) was born in Geneva in 1623, of Italian-exile stock. His father before him and his son after him are numbered among the prominent professors of theology in Calvin's city, and like his father (and Calvin) he was to combine the office of professor with that of pastor. Educated in Geneva and in France, he declined an appointment to the chair of philosophy (often a steppingstone to that of theology) on the ground that it was not his subject, but in the memorable year 1648 he became a professor of theology and held the post until his death in 1687, refusing flattering calls to the Netherlands. His *Institutio theologiae elencticae* appeared in Geneva in 1688, and with the addition of a collection of *Disputationes*, it became the basis of the four-volume *Opera* that enjoyed several reprintings (Utrecht and Amsterdam, 1701; Utrecht, 1734; Edinburgh,

1847). Only fragments have appeared in any translation.[3] But this should not be understood as making him an insignificant figure in the history of theology. Latin was a true international language among Western Christian scholars when he wrote, and for long afterward. In America, knowledge of Latin among serious students of theology was assumed in the nineteenth century, as is witnessed by the freedom and frequency with which Hodge quoted lengthy passages in that tongue, and by the fact that Union Seminary in Richmond kept copies of Turretin's work on hand to enable students to fulfill a reading requirement. Above all, the way in which his theology, and the attitudes embodied in it, entered into the structure of the thought that gave form to much of American piety is evident both from the explicit acknowledgments of influential writers—the Princeton theologians, William G. T. Shedd, and others— and in internal evidence based on the nature of their arguments. From the other side of the Atlantic, a long series of important writers, including Philip Schaff, Heinrich Heppe, Leonard Grensted, and Karl Barth, bears witness to his significance as representative of a long-dominant stratum of Protestant thought.

It is as a Protestant scholastic that Turretin is worth remembering, and few theologians better illustrate the strengths (and weaknesses) of the Reformed aspects of this movement than he does. He comes at its historic climax— the moment when it had made its contribution and run its course.

3. Willson noted this lack when he published a translation of locus 14, questions 10-14, dealing with the atonement (n. 2 above). This translation was reprinted by the Reformed Dutch Church (Reformed Church in America) in 1859, and this edition was reprinted in 1978 (Grand Rapids: Baker). Locus 4, on the decrees of God and especially predestination, is translated in Beardslee, *Reformed Dogmatics.*

Reformed scholasticism may be understood very simply as an effort to develop a biblical theology from the resources of traditional Western Aristotelianism modified by some of the teachings of Peter Ramus, the brash martyr of 1572 who survived in at least the form and methodology of much of the Protestant writing of the next century. All questions, for the scholastic, were approached on the basis of known first principles, which were assumed to be of universal validity and therefore, by true implication, to be present throughout the Bible, since truth cannot contradict truth. This became the dominant form of Reformed theology under the influence of Beza and a series of prolific and influential, although unimaginative, writers who followed him. Even before Beza's influence became decisive, the scholastic method had entered not only the academic but also the practical life of the Reformed churches through the second articles of both the French and the Belgic confessions. By teaching that the true God is really known by reason, however imperfectly, the churches made the continuance of scholasticism inevitable.

As more than one recent writer has noted, Protestant scholasticism arose from the inner realities of the Protestant situation. Given the state of learning and of society at the time, there was no other instrument by which the faith could have articulated itself and defined its stand, for the sake of its own inner needs as well as for the sake of dialogue (or controversy) with those outside. Pietistic withdrawal and indifference to learning and to culture would have been the alternative to Aristotelian scholasticism. One of the marks of the Reformed churches in their formative years was a concern for the total reformation of society and a refusal to be anything less than an establishment force transforming all of society. Humanism, biblicism, and other suggested alternatives to scholasticism were not alternatives. They had not developed the tools for facing the totality of the concerns of society.

The special importance of the doctrine of Scripture within Reformed scholasticism springs first of all from the place of Scripture in Reformed theology. *Sola Scriptura*, like justification by faith, was more than a slogan in Protestantism. It was the basis of what was new, and the heart of what was taught. The absolute supremacy of Scripture colored all else that was said and practiced, no matter what compromises or corruptions were present in practice. Reformed scholasticism was significantly different from Roman Catholic because of this fundamental teaching, and no matter what concessions it made to natural theology, it imposed more definite limitations on the sphere of natural knowledge. The questions of Christian experience and the contemporary work of the Holy Spirit are also present, once and for all, no matter how deeply they are submerged in *a priori* rationalist reasoning. On these matters, Turretin may speak for himself and for the movement through the translation that follows.

What is perhaps the most significant aspect of Turretin's doctrine of Scripture, both theologically and historically, has received little attention. If we focus on Turretin's pastoral interests, we find ourselves in the midst of one of the greatest concerns of the Reformation. Turretin was a pastor as well as a professor, and we are unfortunate in not having any of his sermons, which are said to have been straightforward and practical. It was in any case in the best tradition of the Reformation, from Luther, Zwingli, and Calvin on, that the requirements of the pastoral office be in the forefront of theological activity. And one of the great pastoral concerns, not peculiar to later pietists but integral to the movement, was putting the Bible into the hands of the laity. Much of Turretin's scholasticism can be read as an academic's program for accomplishing this. Much of this locus on Scripture comes to a climax—after the lengthy discussions of authority, canon, text, and translation—in questions 16 – 18 about the perfection, perspicuity, and reading of Scripture. The brevity of question 18 should not be taken as the measure of its importance, for the vindication of the principle set forth in it—that every believer can and should read the Bible without interference—is the vindication of the Protestant movement. The demonstration of the authority of Scripture, the identification of the canon, the question of the reliability of the text and the need for translations, the perfection of Scripture (which, as the reader will see, means its total adequacy for the nourishment of spiritual life), and its perspicuity—all of these are important as a rationale for putting the Bible into the layman's hands, assuring him that with it his spiritual needs are fulfilled, and urging him to read, learn, and trust. Everything that has been said about the need of reliance on Hebrew and Greek and about the necessity of studying the purposes of the original writers has been said, not to enhance the learned professions, but to justify the radical principle that God through Scripture speaks to the believing individual, who needs no church or external judge, but can directly appropriate what is given him. If we consider the form of Turretin's argument, we note that the section about the privilege of reading the Scripture is followed by one about principles of interpretation. The holy, dependable, and understandable Word, in the hands of the believer, is to be read as truth, and a spiritual interpretation is necessary for a spiritual meaning. Allegory is rejected, although the typology that is substituted is, as later experience has shown, subject to abuse. But the effort is always to help the reader find the author's intention, and the presence of figurative language is recognized, although the rules for recognizing it prescribe limitations. This section (question 19) is quite different from the earlier argument about authority, integrity, and perfection. It is less abstract and is of a nature to guide the reader in the practical use of that Bible he has been urged to read. From then on the discussion tends to become anticlimatic, and Turretin finally admits (in question 21) that the subject has been covered, except that the polemics of the age require a few more details.

It was the polemics of the age that gave Turretin's work the final form that it has in many points. Time and again he has indicated that the question hardly needs discussion, but the importunities of adversaries call for refutation.

The effort to justify, once and for all, the vernacular translations and their use by the laity does not, at first glance, appear to be the major thrust of the work. But when it was written, the understanding of the Council of Trent, for better or worse, was such that it seemed the major threat to this basic Protestant principle. The inerrant Bible as a counterweight to the claims of an inerrant pope— such were the terms in which Turretin saw the battle (his "negatives against the *pontificii*" have been rendered "Roman Catholics" rather than "papists"). The trustworthy Bible in the hands of the faithful was the literal, inerrant word on all matters.

The reader of question 20, about the "supreme judge of controversies," will note that although the theologian still relies on excommunication as a means of checking heresy and maintaining ecclesiastical order, he insists that coercion of conscience has no place in Christianity, and that the individual ought to give his consent only to that which God speaking in Scripture assures him is true. The difference between this attitude and that of a medieval inquisitor, burning a relapsed heretic with the assurance that if really repentant the man will still be saved, should be obvious. The medieval doctrine stressed that the individual ought to believe what he learned from the church, as well as to obey.

Turretin and the Protestant states hesitated to implement all the implications of the doctrine. The desire for uniformity as a safeguard for the social order and a confidence that God would give to everyone the same answers, since all use the same created reason, delayed the full introduction of tolerance in theological thinking quite as much as in civil practice. But the doctrine that the individual must submit to God alone and that God speaks to him through Scripture was firmly entrenched in orthodoxy, defended by all the ammunition of the scholastic theology and the ecclesiastical establishment. A major thrust of "orthodoxy," therefore, however latent, was the emphasis on the laymen's use of the Bible.

A very unecclesiastical historian, looking at the Netherlands, states that the new Protestant attitude, which was "difficult to put in words," was expressed "in terms of warfare and afterwards in art."[4] The reference to warfare and art—laymen's activities—is most illuminating with regard to Protestantism in general. The Reformation was in many ways a layman's movement, and Reformed theology in many ways centered in the defense of laymen's rights and the promulgation of laymen's responsibilities, with purposeful Bible reading as basic. The seventeenth century, the golden age of orthodox scholasticism, was one of the great centuries of the Protestant layman,[5] who was remaking culture—one of the aims of the orthodox theology— by taking his Bible-centered faith seriously in his vocation and serving God through his vocation. Warriors like William the Silent (in the sixteenth century), Gustavus Adolphus, and Cromwell have played a prominent role in

4. E. Keble Chatterton, *Old Ship Prints* (New York: Dodd, Mead, 1927), p. 60.
5. See Martin Schmidt in Stephen Neill and Hans Rudi Weber, *The Layman in Christian History* (Philadelphia: Westminster, 1963), chap. 6.

history books. But the new culture was being formed by Milton, Locke, Grotius, Kepler, Boyle, Newton, Rembrandt, Johann Sebastian Bach, and their likes. The theological significance and personal faith of these men have been the subject of considerable study. Many of them, by the standards of their churches, Reformed or Lutheran, were heretics, and some fell short of the moral expectations of common Christianity. But they took the faith, and the injunction to seek God through His Scripture, seriously, and they were followed by a significant succession in the eighteenth and nineteenth centuries. The type of piety involved here is not limited to an intellectual elite; its growth among the "common people" can be recognized, for example, in a line of sturdy English seamen and overseas pioneers that begins in Elizabethan times not only with Sir Humphrey Gilbert but also with John Davis, and finds one high point in the very down-to-the-earth man of the people, Captain James Cook.[6] In twentieth-century America the same succession, in its strength and its weakness, may be observed.

Personal use of the Bible, without ecclesiastical mediation, was the common ground of Lutheran and Reformed, Baptist and Presbyterian, Calvinist and Arminian, and it was the basis on which Protestantism as a religious force came into the new society of post-Renaissance Europe. Whatever reservations and whatever other motivations surrounded it, Reformed scholasticism firmly embraced and defended the principle that the layman not only could, but should, let the Bible speak to him. The establishment of this principle was one of its major thrusts, and Turretin's

6. See Samuel E. Morison, *The European Discovery of America: The Northern Voyages* (New York: Oxford University Press, 1971). For a portrait of Captain Cook as a Christian layman, read the beautiful nonecclesiastical biography by his admirer Alan Villiers, *Captain James Cook* (New York: Scribner, Emblem Editions, 1970), especially the concluding chapter.

locus on Scripture should be read as an expression, in a particular time and place, of a doctrine that was to be of great importance in history and in theological theory, and that remains a living legacy. Equally with the academic Princeton orthodoxy, the self-confident, independent layman is a fruit of his work.

The *oratio funebris* pronounced in Turretin's honor by his distinguished fellow theologian Benedict Pictet was, as would be expected, in conventional "classical" oratorical form, laden with "classical" terms and allusions, some of which would have amazed Cicero. The prayer at the end included the aspiration that the academy might be "the seat of more upright wisdom, the impregnable bulwark of pure truth, the *prytaneum* of righteous souls, the *lararium* of teachers, the compend of the learning of all the world." Pictet added, "May its fame and glory reach the end of the earth, while this church remains the faithful seat of your grace, and of the Ark." Such had been Turretin's ideal—church and school united to the glory of God, and learning as a leading means of making that glory manifest.

This harmony of church and school represented, for Turretin and his colleagues, an aspect of the new society reformed according to the will of God, a society of which the Reformed state church was another aspect or symbol. Both historic understanding and present use of Turretin are advanced by an awareness of the relation of his doctrine of Scripture to subsequent developments in this reformed society.

Turretin's theology assumed that the universality of reason, quite as much as the free action of the Spirit, would lead all inquirers to a similar understanding of biblical truth. In fact the Synod of Dort and the Westminster Assembly established a Reformed version of reason quite as much as a Reformed view of biblical truth, without clearly differentiating philosophical conclusions from biblical faith, although the distinction was recognized in theory. Within the Reformed circle, rather than within all society, conclusions like Turretin's remained definitive.

Even sons of the Reformed tradition, accepting the orthodox invitation to read the Bible and believe what God told them in Scripture, came to conclusions at variance with orthodoxy. Among such were prominent makers of a new world that was emerging, for example, Grotius, Milton, Cromwell, Locke, and Newton. Bible-believing Christians rejected aspects of orthodoxy as firmly as did the more radical (or "faithless") sons of the Reformed church such as Isaac Voss, Pierre Bayle, and Thomas Hobbes. Protestantism, but not Reformed orthodoxy, motivated a new culture whose spiritual pluralism resulted from the success of one thrust of orthodoxy. But this pluralism submerged the hopes of Reformers from Calvin through Turretin, who had seen a new uniformity of obedience to the Word of God as the wave of the future. The new place of the Bible among the laity had explosive results not foreseen in the original teaching.

This inner tension among believers (contemporary with the larger controversies involving Roman Catholics, Lutherans, Anglicans, Reformed, and Anabaptists) was accompanied by an outburst of independent scholarship in history, philology, philosophy, and the new science. Galileo, Kepler, Boyle, Newton, Descartes, Leibniz, and Locke were remaking the whole world of thought and introducing new concepts, replacing some that had long been assumed to be in harmony with the Bible—indeed to be actually taught in it. The gradual abandonment of Ptolemaic astronomy is the best known of these developments; the attrition of the authority of Aristotle (still "the philosopher" for Turretin) is perhaps the most significant. Scholars had, in spite of Francis Bacon and others, accepted not only a world of four elements in which the lighter ones naturally rose to the heavens, but also a whole subconscious outlook about man and nature that the new philosophy-science consciously contradicted. "Reason" no longer taught as Turretin and his friends assumed that it taught. Since truth cannot contradict truth, the new uses of reason posed a problem for Turretin's successors that he had not foreseen. To change one's mind about the interpretation of a biblical statement regarding historical or scientific truth without changing one's mind about a fundamental article of the faith involved hard intellectual work of a kind that he had in theory called for, and that his theology, in its recognition of the validity and necessity of historical and philological research, demands. Ever since his generation, evangelical Christians, like the rest of the world, have been changing their minds about many questions once regarded as settled. Many unnecessary problems have arisen from a misunderstanding of a central issue. The urgency of distinguishing between biblical truth and an interpretation of a biblical statement, especially a historic or scientific one, was seen but not experienced by Turretin. Awareness of this fact today will go far to deliver him from the mere antiquarian or sectarian significance implied by the quotation with which this introduction opened.[7]

This translation is made, with help from George Musgrave Giger's unfinished manuscript at Princeton Theological Seminary, from the Edinburgh edition of 1847, long used in America. On some difficult points I also consulted the Utrecht edition of 1734. The later edition differs in no important respect. I have retained the numbering of para-

---

7. For the question of unchanging truth in the light of new knowledge, see Bernard Ramm, *The Christian View of Science and Scripture* (Grand Rapids: Eerdmans, 1954). On the specific question of the philosophical drift away from Aristotle and its effect on all European thought, see John Dillenberger, *Protestant Thought and Natural Science* (Garden City, NY: Doubleday, 1960), chap. 8.

graphs ("theses"). I have modified some biblical citations to conform to the Revised Standard Version, and where biblical citations differ from the verse numbering of the English Bible, I have so indicated. The footnotes are mine. In the body of the translation everything, including the matter in parentheses, is from the original except what is enclosed in brackets. Because of the difficulty of obtaining the original text, I have at some points been free in including Latin and Greek words from the original, where this original might clarify the translation. Turretin's Latin sentences are long and "Germanic," often with Greek words incorporated into them. I have at times made radical changes in the sentence structure but have sought faithful translation rather than elegant English.

Thanks are due to the publisher and to my family for their patience, to my colleagues at New Brunswick Theological Seminary for their support, and to Ms. Darcy Lovgren for typing from my manuscript.

The Necessity
of Verbal Revelation

QUESTION **1** Was revelation by the word necessary? (Affirmative)

I. Since the word of God is the unique foundation (*principium*) of theology, its necessity is properly investigated at the very beginning: was it necessary for God to reveal himself to us by the word? or, was the word of God necessary? There have been in the past, and are also today, some who maintain that sufficient capacity for living well and happily resides in human nature, so that they regard any revelation from heaven as not only superfluous, but even as absurd. Since nature takes care of the needs of people just as it does those of other living creatures, so, they believe, reason, or the light of nature, is fully sufficient for the guidance of life and the pursuit of happiness.

II. But the orthodox church has always believed very differently, declaring that the revelation of God's word is absolutely and simply necessary to humanity for salvation because [the word] is the seed which causes rebirth (I Peter 1:23), the lamp by which we are guided (Ps. 119:105), the food by which we are nourished (Heb. 5:13 – 14), and the foundation upon which we depend (Eph. 2:20).

III. The following evidence proves the above: (1) the supreme goodness of God, communicative of itself;[1] since he has created mankind for himself, that is, for a supernatural end, and for a condition far happier than this earthly existence, he cannot be conceived as willing that they should lack in this respect, but he made clear to them by means of the word this very happiness and the way for obtaining it, which ["natural"] reason did not know. (2) The extreme blindness and corruption of people, who, although after sin still have some residual light for guidance in earthly and mundane affairs, yet in divine and heavenly matters which concern blessedness (*felicitas*) are so blind and depraved that they can neither know anything of the truth, nor perform anything of the good, except through the initiative of God (I Cor. 2:14; Eph. 5:8). (3) Right reason, which teaches that God can be known and worshiped for salvation only through the light of God, just as the sun can be seen by us only through its own light (Ps. 36:10). Nor would impostors who have devised new religions have invented their conversations with divine beings or with angels, as Numa Pompilius did with the nymph Aegeria, or Mohammed with Gabriel, unless everybody was convinced that the correct form of worship of the divine being depended on his own revelation. Thus the common opinion of all nations, even of barbarians, is that for the welfare of humanity there is needed, besides that reason that they call the guide of life, some heavenly wisdom. This [conviction] gave rise to the various religions that are scattered about the globe. In this connection those who maintain that these religions are merely ingenious human schemes for uniting people in civic responsibilities are not to be believed. It will be granted that it is certain that many

1. Turretin here follows his usual procedure of assuming that any accepted theological truth can be introduced as proof in any portion of the argument. He has not yet discussed the goodness of God, but will do so in locus 3 (*De Deo*), question 20.

clever men have manipulated religion in order to instill reverence into the common people, as a means of keeping their spirits submissive, but they could never have accomplished this unless there was already inborn (*ingenitus*) in the human mind a sense of its own ignorance and helplessness, by which the more readily people were led astray by those vagabonds and quacks.

IV. A double appetite which is implanted in mankind by nature—the longing both for truth and for immortality—confirms this. The one desire is to know the truth; the other, to enjoy the highest good. As the intellect is brought to perfection by the contemplation of truth, the will is brought to perfection by the enjoyment of the good, of which the blessed life consists. Since it is impossible that these two appetites should be in vain,[2] revelation, which makes evident, as nature cannot, both the primal truth and the highest good, and the path to both of them, was necessary. Finally, the glory of God and the salvation of mankind demand revelation, because the school of nature cannot lead us to the true God and to legitimate worship of him, nor can it disclose the plan (*ratio*) of salvation, by which people may escape from the wretchedness of sin to the state of perfect bliss which exists in union with God. The higher school of grace was therefore necessary, in which God teaches us true religion by his word, to establish us in the knowledge and worship of himself, and to lead us to the enjoyment of eternal salvation in communion with him, to which neither philosophy nor any human effort (*ratio*) can attain.

V. Granted that in the works of creation and providence God manifests himself clearly, so that "what can be known about God is plain to them [men]" and his invisible nature

2. Turretin regularly assumes that it is contrary to the nature of any created being for its potentialities to be unrealizable.

has been clearly perceived from the creation of the world (Rom. 1:19 – 20), this real revelation cannot suffice for salvation after sin,[3] not only in the subjective sense, because it has not, as an accompaniment, the power of the Spirit, by which human blindness and evil are corrected; but also in the objective sense, because it contains nothing concerning the mysteries of salvation, and God's mercy in Christ, without whom there is no salvation (Acts 4:12). What can be known about God is indeed presented, but not what is to be believed.[4] God is known from the work of creation as creator, but not as redeemer; his power and divinity, that is, the existence of the divine being (*numen*) and his unlimited power (*virtus*) [are known], but not his grace and saving mercy. It was therefore necessary to make up the deficiency of the prior revelation, which, because of the sin that had been committed, was useless and inadequate, by another one, more splendid not only in degree but also in kind, that God might use not only a silent teacher, but also open his sacred mouth, that he could not only make known his more wonderful power, but also disclose the mystery of his will for our salvation.

VI. Although natural theology deals with various matters concerning God and his properties, his will and his works, it does not, without the supernatural revelation of the word, teach us that understanding of God which can serve for salvation. It shows that God is and what he is like, both in unity of essence and in the nature of some attributes, but it does not show who he is, either in his personal unity

3. The language emphasizes that natural revelation is real revelation—even the imperfect knowledge of God depends on God. *Post peccatum* means "after [Adam's] sin" in a chronological sense, as the tenses in Turretin's Latin clearly show, but also, more generally, "as a result of sin."

4. The sentence contrasts τὸ γνωστόν and τὸ πιστόν, the content of knowledge and the content of faith, in a form that is easily subject to the "scholastic" interpretation that makes faith a matter of accepting verbal formulae.

(*in individua*) or with regard to the persons [of the Trinity]. ["Natural revelation"] shows God's will with regard to the law, imperfectly and obscurely (Rom. 2:14 – 15), but the mystery of the gospel is entirely lacking in it. It proclaims the works of creation and providence (Ps. 19; Acts 14:17; Rom. 1:19 – 20). But it does not rise to the works of redemption and grace, which can become known to us only by the word (Rom. 10:17; 16:25 – 26).

The Necessity
of Scripture

QUESTION **2** Was it necessary for the word to be committed to writing? (Affirmative)

I. Since in the preceding question we have proved the necessity of the word, in this one the necessity of Scripture, or the written word, is argued against the Roman Catholics. For, just as to establish more easily their traditions and unwritten teachings, and the authority of their supreme pontiff, they strive earnestly to denigrate the authority of Scripture, they also try, in more ways than one, to disparage its necessity. They call it useful for the church, but not necessary, as Bellarmine argues in *De Verbo Dei*, book 4, chapter 4. Cardinal Hosius even utters such blasphemy as to say, "It would have been a better situation for the church if no Scripture at all had ever existed," and Valentia says, "It would have been more convenient had it not been written."

II. With regard to the state of the question, let it be noted that "Scripture" may be understood in two ways—either *materialiter* with regard to the teaching transmitted, or *formaliter* with regard to the writing and form of transmission. In the first sense we regard it to be simply and absolutely necessary, as said above, so that the church can never live without it. But in the second sense, which is here under discussion, we acknowledge that it is not absolutely necessary on God's part because, just as he taught the church by the spoken word alone for two thousand years before Moses, so, if he had wished, he could have taught it later the same way. But [Scripture] is necessary hypothetically[1] on account of the divine will, since it seemed good to God, for weighty reasons, to commit his word to writing. For this reason [Scripture] has, by divine ordinance, been made so necessary that it pertains not only to the well-being of the church, but to its very being, so that now the church cannot exist without the Scripture. Therefore, God is not bound to the Scripture, but has bound us to it.

III. The question, therefore, is not whether the writing of the word is absolutely and simply necessary, but whether it is necessary *secundum quid* on account of the hypothesis; not for every age, but for the present age and circumstances; not in relation to God's power and freedom, but in relation to his wisdom and to the economy of his dealing with the human race. For, just as in the economy of the natural order parents change their manner of dealing with their children as these grow older, so that infants are first directed by the spoken word, then by the voice of a teacher and the reading of books, and finally are freed from the guidance of the teacher and learn on their own from books, so the heavenly Father, who instructs his people as the head of a family (Deut. 8:5), taught the church, when it was still young and childish, by the spoken word, the most simple form of revelation. Then, as it began to mature and was established under the law in its early youth, he taught both by the spoken word, because of continuing

---

1. *Ex hypothesi* (i.e., under the conditions established), in this case, by God's free action.

childishness, and by writing, because of the beginnings of maturity, until the apostles' time. But when [the church] had reached adulthood, under the gospel, he wanted it to be satisfied with the most perfect form of revelation, that is, the written light. Therefore, Scripture is necessary not only by the necessity of a commandment, but also by the hypothesis of the divine economy, which God wanted to be varied and manifold in the different ages of the church (Eph. 3:10).

IV. The distinction between the word as written and as unwritten has arisen because of this process. This is not, as Roman Catholics hold, the division of a genus into species, as if the written word differed from the unwritten, but it is the division of the subject into its accidents, because the same Word is always involved; it was once unwritten, but now has been written. It is therefore called "unwritten," not with respect to the present, but to past time, when God chose to teach his church by a spoken word, not by writing.

V. Although God formerly spoke to the fathers "in many and various ways" (Heb. 1:1), sometimes by an audible voice, sometimes by internal and nonsensory action, sometimes in dreams and visions, sometimes taking the appearance of human form, often using the ministry of angels and other appropriate means, yet the teaching was always the same, and was not changed either by the form of revelation and transmission or by changing times.[2]

VI. Three [needs] in particular support the necessity of Scripture: (1) the preservation of the word; (2) its defense; (3) its proclamation. It was necessary for the written word to be given to the church to be the fixed and changeless

2. Two main points have been made—first, that God's decision to reveal in the written word rests on his unconditioned good pleasure but is part of his rational plan; second, that the content of revelation is always the same (so no unwritten tradition contrary to Scripture can possibly be revelation).

rule of faith of the true religion, which could thus more readily be preserved pure and whole in spite of the weakness of memory, the perversity of humanity, and the shortness of life; more surely defended against the frauds and corruptions of Satan, and more readily proclaimed and transmitted not only to people who were scattered and separated from one another, but to future generations as well. As Vives reminds us (*De causis corruptium artium 1*), "By letters all the arts are preserved as in a treasury, so that they can never be lost, although transmission by hand is uncertain." "Divine and marvelous is this blessing of letters," says Quintilian, "which protects words and holds them like a deposit for an absent person." Nor are the statutes and edicts of kings and commonwealths inscribed in bronze or posted in public places for any other reason than that this is the surest means of preserving them in their original form, and of proclaiming throughout the ages matters which it is important for people to know.

VII. Although before Moses the church did without the written word, it does not follow that it can do so now, for the situation of the infant church of those days, which did not yet form a numerous body, was very different from that of the present church, which is established and of large size. The church of former times differed from that of later days: in it the unwritten word could more easily be preserved because of the longevity of the patriarchs, the small number of covenant people, and the frequency of revelations (even if many of them underwent corruption). But in another age, when human life had been shortened, and the church was not limited to one or another family, but had increased to a very large company, and the divine oracles were more rarely given, another form of governance was called for, so that this sacred commonwealth was ruled not merely by the spoken word, but by written laws.

VIII. Although some individual churches may have been without the written word of God at some particular time, especially when they were first established, they were not without what was written in the Word of God, which certainly sounded in their ears through human ministry; nor did the church as a whole lack the Scripture.

IX. The Holy Spirit as helper (ἐπιχορηγία),[3] by whom believers are to be taught by God (Jer. 31; John 6:43[45]; I John 2:27), does not make the Scripture any less necessary, because (1) he is not given us to bring new revelations, but to impress the written word on our hearts, so that the Word can never be separated from the Spirit (Isa. 59:21). The Word acts objectively; the Spirit, efficiently. The Word strikes the ears externally; the Spirit lays bare the heart, internally. The Spirit is the teacher; Scripture is the teaching that he gives us. (2) The words in Jeremiah 31 and I John 2:27 are not to be understood absolutely and simply, as if it were no longer necessary for believers, under the new covenant, to use the Scripture; if this were so, there would have been no point in John's writing to them. But they are to be understood in a relative sense, because, on account of the greater abundance of the Holy Spirit under the new covenant, believers were not to be taught in so burdensome a form as through the primitive and undeveloped elements of the old. (3) Jeremiah's promise will receive its complete fulfillment only in heaven, where, on account of the brilliant vision of God, there will no longer be need for the ministry of Scripture or of pastors, but everyone will see God directly, face to face.

X. It is not true that the church was preserved without Scripture during the Babylonian captivity, for Daniel is said to have perceived, from the books, before the end of the seventy-year period, the number of the years (Dan. 9:2),

3. Philippians 1:19.

and in Nehemiah 8:2, Ezra is said to bring forth the book of the laws, not to write it anew. IV Esdras [II Esdras] 4:23,[4] being apocryphal, proves nothing. Even if Ezra gathered the sacred books into one corpus, and corrected the careless errors of scribes, it does not follow that the church had completely lacked Scripture [in his time].[5]

XI. There is no evidence for Bellarmine's assumption that, since the time of Moses, any from other nations who have been led to the true religion had tradition only, and lacked Scripture, for if any became proselytes, they were instructed thoroughly in Moses and the prophets, as the single example of the eunuch of Queen Candace in Acts 8 [26 – 39] proves adequately. Nor was Scripture completely unknown to the Gentiles, especially after it was translated into Greek in the time of Ptolemy Philadelphus.

XII. Christ therefore is our only teacher (Matt. 23:8) in such a way that the ministry of Scripture is not excluded, but is included of necessity, because he now speaks to us in it only, and builds us up through it. Nor is Christ opposed to Scripture, but to the false teachers of the Pharisees, who ambitiously pretended to the magisterial authority that belongs to Christ alone.

XIII. Although formally Scripture has no personal value for illiterates, who cannot read, nevertheless it serves materially for their instruction and edification, inasmuch as the teaching which goes on in the church is not taken from any other source.

4. "The unwritten covenants no longer exist."

5. Turretin is prepared to give Ezra a place in the preservation of Scripture, but not to accept the apocryphal account given in II Esdras 14:19 – 22, which he does not mention, but which clearly lies behind the teaching that he rejects.

The Divine Imperative
of Written Revelation

QUESTION **3**

> Was the Holy Scripture written because of the circumstances of the time (*occasionaliter*) and without divine command? (Negative, against the Roman Catholics)

I. This question is debated between us and the Roman Catholics, who, in order to minimize the authority and perfection of Scripture, teach not only that it is less than necessary, and that the church could do without it, but even that it was written without any express divine commandment, and simply passed on to the church as a result of special circumstances. [They also] teach that Christ gave the apostles no commandment to write, and that they had no intention of writing the gospel, except in a secondary sense and because of special circumstances, as Bellarmine argues (*De Verbo Dei*, book 4, 3 − 4).

II. That the sacred writers responded to circumstances of time and place is unquestioned. We do not deny that they often put the mysteries of God into writing under such influence. The question is whether they wrote under such circumstances that they did not write by divine revelation and commandment. We indeed hold that this is not a matter of opposition, but of combination. They could write under the influence of circumstances and at the same time from divine commandment and inspiration. Indeed, since such a circumstance was not presented to them except through divine action, the writing was in accordance with the divine commandment, and the situation neither arose without design (*temere*) nor was used of their own will (*sponte*).

III. An implicit and general commandment is to be distinguished from an explicit and special one. Granted that all the sacred writers did not have a special commandment to write, although this is frequent (Exod. 17[:14]; Deut. 31:19; Isa. 8:1; Jer. 36:2; Hab. 2:2; Rev. 1:12[11]), yet they all had the general one. For the commandment to teach (Matt. 28:19) includes the commandment to write, since without writing we cannot teach those who are in another place or who come after us, whence preaching is said to be done in writing, in deed, and in word. Further, immediate inspiration and the internal direction by which they were led by the Holy Spirit were the equivalent of a commandment (*loco mandati*) for the sacred writers, so that Paul called Scripture "God-breathed" (II Tim. 3:16), and Peter said, "Prophecy did not come by the will of man, but men of God spoke, moved by the Holy Spirit" (II Peter 1:21): that is, the apostles wrote when God inspired and moved them, although not in a mechanical manner, under coercion. No more effective commandment could be given than by the inspiration of the things to be written, nor is any one of the promises made by ambassadors fulfilled except one they have been commanded to make.

IV. Granted that the apostles do not always mention a special commandment of Christ, which however they often do (for instance, John, Jude, and others), yet they witness strongly enough to such a commandment (1) when they professed themselves to be universal teachers of all nations, (2) when they called themselves faithful servants of Christ, and therefore peculiarly anxious to carry out his commandments, (3) when they witness that they were guided by the Spirit (II Peter 1:21). Therefore, Gregory sums the matter up well: "He who uttered these words wrote them; he who was the inspirer of their works wrote them."

v. Not all the apostles were required to write, although all were required to preach. As they were jointly sent of divine inspiration to the task of preaching, so they should all proclaim the same message and follow it with writing; there was an equal responsibility in all matters that were essential for the apostolate, since all were equal as God-breathed teachers. But they did not have equal responsibility in the performance of every particular action, so it is not strange if, through the freedom of the Holy Spirit, some were called to both preaching and writing, and others to preaching only.

VI. A single book was not put together by all the apostles conjointly, both so that they would not seem to have acted together in conspiracy, and so that it might not seem to have greater authority than what each one wrote individually; it would seem that for the same reason Christ refrained altogether from writing: that we might say that he is the one who wrote his teaching not with ink but by the Spirit of the living God, not on tablets but in the heart (II Cor. 3:2[− 3]). It was therefore sufficient that that which was approved by all [the apostles] should be written by some of them. Indeed it adds much weight and authority to the apostolic writings that, although they were written in different places, for different purposes and circumstances, in different styles and different forms, addressed to different people, yet [they] are so harmonious.

VII. It was not necessary for a catechism to be written by the apostles; (1) it was sufficient for them to transmit that by which all symbolic books and catechisms were to be tested. (2) If they did not write a catechism formally, yet materially they passed on, both in the Gospels and in the

Epistles, that from which we may do catechetical work in the best possible manner.

VIII. As we ought not to impose law on the Holy Spirit, and prescribe to him the method of revealing his will, so we ought not to doubt that the form of writing that has been followed is the most suitable, not only because at that time teaching by means of letters was a widely accepted procedure, because this manner of teaching was most useful for spreading the gospel rapidly, which was the chief purpose of the apostles; but also because this simple and popular form of writing suits the capacities of all, the uneducated as well as the educated, and teaches a theology that is not ideal and merely theoretical, but practical and specific (*in hypothesi*).

IX. The Apostles' Creed is so called, not efficiently because it was passed on by the apostles, but materially, because it was composed from the apostolic teaching, and is the kernel (*medulla*) and compendium of the apostolic teaching.

X. Those who wrote under the influence and compulsion (*necessitas*)[1] of circumstances could nevertheless be writing from a [special] commandment: two realities, one of which is subordinate to the other, ought not to be understood as contradictory. Christ's commandment was the primary activating cause and the circumstance a secondary, less significant (*minus principalis*) activating cause, by which, as they wrote for the glory of God and the edification of the neighbor, the apostles preached both from divine commandment and on account of circumstances.

1. The theological importance of question 3 is obvious. Turretin sees the importance of a doctrine that will combine divine inspiration with the fullness of the human personality of the inspired person. His use of such words as "necessity" is never to be understood mechanistically. It is worthwhile to compare this passage with his treatment of predestination and freedom in locus 4, especially question 4, translated in Beardslee, *Reformed Dogmatics* (Grand Rapids: Baker, 1977), pp. 348 – 351.

XI. Granted that it was proper for the apostles to write because they were under obligation to teach, it does not follow that pastors are now always under the same obligation to write as to teach, because they work under different conditions. The apostles were obligated to teach all nations, as ecumenical teachers, but this is not the case with ordinary pastors, who have a particular congregation (*grex*) committed to them.

The Authority
of Scripture

QUESTION **4** Are the Holy Scriptures genuine and divine?
(Affirmative)

I. The question of the authority (*authoritas*) of Scripture depends upon its origin, which has just been discussed. Since it is from God, it cannot be other than genuine (*authenticus*) and divine.[1] Hence arises the question of its authority, which can have two aspects: (1) with atheists and pagans (*ethnici*), who grant to Scripture no more authority than to any other writing; (2) with Christians who, while acknowledging [its authority], understand it as depending, at least in our understanding (*quoad nos*), on the testimony of the church. With the first, it must be asked whether Holy Scriptures are credible in themselves and divine; with the second, how this is made known to us, or

1. The use of the adjective *divinus*, and, more rarely, the noun *divinitas*, to refer to Scripture could be misleading. It is to be noted (paragraph 6 below) that Turretin calls Scripture "the effluence of the Father." His theology includes a view of God as "the all by way of eminence," and he regards the attributes of God as not differing from the essence (3.5). So Scripture, the Word of God, is a sort of continuum of the second person of the Trinity, and, although not inspired in a mechanical manner (question 3 above), is nevertheless in all respects true, a statement which, in the absolute sense, applies only to God. Note what is said about historical statements (paragraph 4), and about words (paragraph 5).

on what testimony, above all, the authority of Scripture depends. Here we are discussing the first question, not the second.

II. Granted that in truth the first question seems hardly necessary among Christians, where it should be assumed without controversy that Scripture is God-breathed and the primary foundation of the faith, yet because there are even today among Christians too many atheists and libertines who seek in every way to erode this most sacred truth,[2] it is of first importance for salvation that we protect our faith fully against the demonic scoffing of such irreligious folk.

III. The authority of Scripture, concerning which we are now writing, is nothing else than the right and dignity of the sacred books, by which those articles which are set forth in them to be believed are most worthy of faith, and those which are set forth as to be left undone or to be done demand obedience. The basis is the divine and infallible truth of the books, which have God as author, because he has the supreme privilege of binding mankind to faith and obedience. This can be either intrinsic or extrinsic. The first is the worthiness of faith of the Word in itself, which is always the same and which rests upon itself, whether human testimony supports it or not. The second is the opinion or judgment of people concerning Scripture, which differs by reason of the difference between subjects [persons].

IV. Further, authority (*authentia*) is either that of history and narration, or that of truth and the norm. According to the former whatever is told in Scripture is true as it is told, whether good or evil, true or false. The latter refers to mat-

2. Turretin rarely names these contemporary "atheists and libertines." Apparently those who introduced the philosophical methodology of doubt into theology (i.e., Cartesians) are so regarded (1.13.14), as well as some aspects of Hobbes's teaching. He also mentions Gassendi as a reviver of Epicurus (11.1.6).

ters true in themselves, that are communicated as the norm of faith and morals. Not everything in Scripture has the authority of a norm, inasmuch as words of blasphemous people and of the devil are recorded, but everything has the authority of historical truth.

v. It is not a question of whether the sacred writers simply as human beings and in private matters would err. We readily concede this. Nor is it a question whether they could err as holy men led by the Holy Spirit, and in the substance, the total message. This I suppose no one of our adversaries, except a defender of pure atheism, will uphold. The question is whether in writing they were so led and inspired by the Holy Spirit that, with regard to both the substance and the words, their writings were authoritative (*authenticus*) and divine. The adversaries deny this; we affirm it.

vi. Scripture shows itself to be divine, in an authoritative manner and by means of an artless argument or testimony, when it calls itself "God-breathed." This testimony can be used with profit in disputes among Christians, who themselves profess to accept [Scripture], but not against others who reject it. But Scripture [also shows itself to be divine] rationally (*ratiocinative*) by means of arguments constructed by reason, based on marks (*notae*) which God has impressed on Scripture, which carry before them the unquestionable proofs (*argumenta*) of divinity. For just as the works of God proclaim the incomparable excellence of their creator, seen in certain qualities perceived by the eyes, and as the sun becomes known by its own light, even so [God] wills that various rays of divinity, by which he may be recognized, should flow out from Scripture, which is the effluence of the Father of lights and the sun of righteousness.

vii. These marks are both extrinsic and intrinsic. The former, although they are insufficient for a full proof of the matter, nevertheless are of great weight for confirming it, and convincing those who deny it. [But] it is in the latter that the chief strength of the argument lies.

VIII. The external marks are: (1) the origin [of Scripture]: its primal antiquity surpassing all pagan monuments; as Tertullian said, "Whatever is first is most true"; (2) its survival (*duratio*): the wonders of the divine Word through the provision for its protection against the most powerful and hostile enemies who sought to destroy it by sword and fire, right down to the present day, while a multitude of other books, against which nothing of the kind was attempted, have been altogether lost; (3) its agents and writers, who showed the greatest candor and sincerity in writing, and did not conceal their failures, but openly avowed them; (4) its adjuncts: the number, constancy, and condition of the martyrs, who sealed it with their blood. For since nothing is dearer to people than life, so many myriads of both sexes, and of all ages and walks of life, could not have so willingly gone forth to death, even in its most cruel forms, in defense of Scripture, unless they were convinced of its divinity. Nor would God have cared to exercise his omnipotence in the performing of so many and great miracles as were performed, both under the law and under the gospel, for producing faith in the divinity of Scripture, if it were merely a product of human intellect. In addition there is the testimony of adversaries themselves, as that of the pagans to Moses, of Josephus and the authors of the Talmud to Christ, and of Mohammed to both Testaments, which can be found in the writings of Vives, Plessaeus, Grotius, and others. Finally there is the consensus of [Christian] people, who, although they differ concerning religious teaching, worship, language, and behavior, yet receive this Word as a most precious treasury of divine truth, and hold it as the foundation of religion and the worship of God; nor is it credible that God would have permitted such a multitude of people, who sought him earnestly, to be deceived for so long by lying books.[3]

IX. The internal marks, which are more significant, are also of many kinds. (1) The content (*materia*): the awe-inspiring sublimity of the mysteries such as the Trinity, the incarnation, the satisfaction of Christ, the resurrection of the dead, and others, which could not be found out by the wisdom of any mind; the holiness and purity of the commandments, which bring (*cogo*) into order the very meditations and inward desires of the heart and are fit to make people perfect in every form of virtue, and worthy of God; the certainty of the prophecies (*oracula*) concerning the most hidden and distant matters. Knowledge and prediction of the future, depending on the will of God alone, is unique to God (*Numen*)[4] (Isa. 41:23). (2) The style: the divine majesty, appearing no less in the simplicity than in the gravity, and that absolute uncompromising manner of laying obligation upon all without distinction—on both the exalted and the humble. (3) The form: the divine consensus and total harmony, not only between the Testaments, with the fulfillment of prediction and typology, but also between individual books of both Testaments, so much the more amazing in that these books were the work of many authors, who wrote at different times and places, so that they were unable to confer with one another about the matters on which they wrote. (4) The purpose: the aim of everything toward the glory of the one God and the holiness and salvation of humanity. (5) The effect: the light

3. The looseness of the argument shows that the author took seriously what he said about the relative insignificance of these external marks. He includes material which is hardly a mark of Scripture at all, but omits nothing that might serve his argument. Here he is a preacher as much as an academic.

4. Turretin usually uses the common *Deus* for God. The occasional use of *Numen* may be stylistic. Here it is obviously the God of Scripture, whom he also calls "Jehovah," not merely some divine being of natural theology.

and efficacy of the divine teaching, which, with more penetrating power than a two-edged sword, pierces into the very soul, engenders faith and piety in the minds of hearers, and unfailing constancy for confessors, and always come forth triumphant from the reign of Satan and false religions. These criteria are truly such that they cannot apply to any human writings, all of which bear the evidence of human weakness, but they truly show that Scripture is divine, especially when they are taken, not one at a time, but altogether.

X. It is not to be thought that these marks appear in equal force in all the books of Scripture. Just as one star differs from another in brilliance, so in this heaven of Scripture some books send forth more glorious and plentiful rays, others fewer and more meager ones, depending on whether they are more or less necessary for the church, and contain teachings of greater or less importance. This brilliance shines forth much more in the Gospels and the Epistles of Paul than in the Books of Ruth and Esther, but it is nonetheless certain that those evidences of truth and majesty, which prove them divine and authoritative in themselves, are in all of them, or at least that nothing is found in them that makes their authority doubtful.

XI. It is not necessary that there should be these marks in every pericope or verse of the canonical books, or in particular parts of Scripture, separated from the whole, those marks by which they can be distinguished from the Apocrypha. It is enough that they are present in the divine writings considered together and as a whole.

XII. Granted that false religions are accustomed to use these criteria to vindicate their teaching, yet nonetheless the true one may ascribe them to itself, for the false opinion of human beings does not destroy the truth. Nor will a believer be unable truly to proclaim the divine quality of the Holy Scripture, in which he sees everywhere the most brilliant rays of divine truth, [merely] because a Turk falsely attributes this divine quality (*divinitas*) to his Qur'an, or a Jew attributes it to his Cabala, because the fictions and lies of which both books are altogether composed are obvious.

XIII. Although faith rests on the authority of testimony, and not on scientific demonstration, it does not follow that it cannot be supported by intellectual arguments at times, especially when faith is first formed, because faith, before it believes, should (*debere*)[5] have the clearly perceived divine quality of the witness whom it should believe, [known] from sure marks found in [the witness]; otherwise it cannot believe him. For where such grounds for believing anyone are lacking, the testimony of such a witness is not worthy of belief.

XIV. The witness of the prophets and apostles is superior to all objection, and cannot be questioned by reason. For, if it were uncertain and fallible, this would be either because they were deceived or because they wished to deceive others, but neither can be said. (1) They were not deceived, nor could they have been. For if they were deceived, they were deceived either by another or by themselves. The former cannot be said, for [they were not deceived] either by God, who, just as he can be deceived by no one likewise cannot deceive anyone,[6] nor by unfallen angels, nor by demons, since this teaching leads to the

5. Our generation's questions were of course not in Turretin's mind, but *debeo* (ought, must) refers both to the psychological impossibility of trusting one who does not appear trustworthy, and the moral impropriety of trusting on grounds not personally understood or experienced—the constant Protestant polemic against "implicit faith." Both "cannot" (subjectively) and "should not" (morally) are therefore implied.

6. The whole section is constructed by the traditional scholastic method of dividing the question. The truthfulness of unfallen angels, and of God, is regarded as not requiring proof here. In later portions of the work, both topics are presented at length. Here Turretin says that God *non potest* deceive anyone, indicating an objective and absolute impossibility.

total destruction of the kingdom of the devil. [That they deceived themselves] is no more possible, for if anyone is deceived about any event, it is mainly either because he did not see it himself but heard from others whom he trusted, or because he saw it incidentally and in passing, or because it is obscure and too difficult for human understanding, or because the person is of impaired mind and limited by some pathological condition because of which he interprets poorly. But in this case nothing of this sort took place. For (1) they reported what they knew not by doubtful report or from others who knew imperfectly, but what they themselves knew by the most certain and experiential knowledge, since they were witnesses by eye and ear, in matters in the comprehension of which they were engaged with earnest concern and zeal. (2) Nor did they speak of remote and distant affairs, but of events which happened in their own time and in the place in which they wrote, as is written, "What we have seen with our eyes, what we have heard concerning the word of life, tht we proclaim" (I John 1:1 – 2). (3) It is not a question of matters that were obscure or that rested on mere speculation, concerning which simple and uneducated people, not comprehending their sublimity, might easily have been deceived, but of events that took place in their presence and before their eyes: for example, the resurrection of Christ, of whom, before his death, they were regular companions, and who had shown himself openly to them after his resurrection, not in passing, but for a significant amount of time, not once, but often, not before one or another individual, but before many of both sexes, and all walks of life. (4) Finally, it cannot be said that their faculties were impaired; for not only is there no distorted imagination or disturbed mind, but rather they give evidence of wisdom and sound mind in both word and life; and furthermore not one or another individual but many people experience and report the same thing. From this it follows that there is no reason why they can be said to have been deceived.

xv. [2] But, just as they were not deceived, neither did they wish to deceive. For those who deceive and lie have in mind some gain from lying and deception, either to receive honor (*gloria*), or the gratitude of the human race, or to gain wealth and ease. But what reward, either in life or in death, was sought by the men of God when they proclaimed this testimony? While alive, they often experienced on its account the very fate by which people are driven to deception—poverty, exile, crucifixion, and extreme torture—and, after death, infamy and everlasting loss.[7] Nevertheless, disregarding such considerations, they, knowing the risk, did not hesitate to meet ultimate decisions for the sake of confirming their witness, and, forever dying, to undergo the most bitter humiliation and suffering. Who could believe that they would have been willing to bear all this for the sake of something they knew to be doubtful or false, when it was known for a certainty that anyone who took their course would meet loss of reputation and property, if not death? No one, surely, can argue that they were so enamored of a desire for lying that they did it in a manner at once most stupid and evil; most stupid, that they should want to lie not for their advantage but most certainly for their disadvantage, when they wrote against their very religion itself, which so strictly forbids lying; most evil, because in lying they would have sought to deceive the whole world, and, with no advantage for themselves, to involve everyone in evil with them.[8]

---

7. *Poena aeterna,* a curious description of the fate of Christian martyrs. I have taken *poena* in the general sense of "compensation," but it is possible that the phrase was a lapse on the writer's part.

8. The paragraph comes close to special pleading, and illustrates the fact that Turretin, even in writing apologetics, finds it difficult to adopt any but a Christian point of view.

XVI. Further, they could not have deceived, even if they wanted to. For they did not write of events that were remote and separated from their experience, or which took place before their time, or secretly and in some corner in the absence of witnesses, as those who impose on the masses commonly do, nor could they easily have conspired in falsehood. But they described events which took place in their own time, in public and in the light of day (*coram sole*),[9] in the very place where they wrote, and indeed which often concerned those who had seen and heard what they wrote about, who would readily have detected fraud and deceit, if they were present. If, therefore, they were not deceived and did not deceive, there is no doubt but that their witness is sacred (*divinus*), and that all teaching that depends on it is authoritative (*authenticus*).

XVII. That the prophets and apostles were such, and that they wrote the books attributed to them, cannot be called in question without destroying all belief in historical records (*antiquitatis fides*), and giving rise to total scepticism (*Pyrrhonismus*). It is just as possible to raise the question with regard to all other books that have survived, but since it is certain that these books were written by some authors, what sane person would not more readily believe that they were written by those whose names they bear, as the Christian church everywhere has always held, and over which no controversy has been begun either by Jews or by pagans, and which in the earliest times, when it was possible to know the facts, was already accepted, than [to believe that they were written] by somebody else?

XVIII. Anything that can be brought up to destroy faith in the Mosaic history can easily be refuted if examined in detail. For (1) if anyone should deny that Moses ever ex-

9. *Coram sole;* cf. the phrase *under the sun* in Ecclesiastes.

isted, or was the author of the books ascribed to him, he could be shown wrong without difficulty, both because not only Jews and Christians but also many profane writers acknowledge him, and also because [his authorship] has always been accepted by a multitude of people, nor can it be questioned on any ground unless we wish to overthrow historical belief altogether, and to deny that Plato, Aristotle, Cicero, and others ever lived and wrote the books that bear their names, which no one except a demented person would maintain. Much less can this be maintained with regard to Moses than with regard to these others, because there is no book which the Jews would have had more reason to throw away, since by so doing they would have freed themselves from the yoke of a most burdensome law. But on the contrary, none has been received and preserved by them with greater care and enthusiasm, nor accorded, contrary to expectation, such authority, as it has been regarded as divine law and the norm of religion; certainly (*sane*) for no other reason than conviction concerning the truth contained in it.

XIX. (2) Secondly, if anyone, convinced by another, gives up this point and admits that Moses lived and wrote the books attributed to him, but maintains that he was an outstanding impostor and falsifier, who deceived the Israelite people by empty lies and false miracles (*prodigii*), and subjected them to himself by means of the law which he proclaimed, such a person can be refuted no less easily. For, not to mention that the pagans themselves, and irreconcilable opponenets like Porphyry (*Adversus Christianos*, book 4),[10] give praise to Moses as a truthful writer, it cannot

---

10. This is Turretin's citation. See T. W. Crafer, "The Work of Porphyry against the Christians and Its Reconstruction," *Journal of Theological Studies* XV (1914), pp. 360 – 395, 481 – 512; James Moffatt, "Great Attacks on Christianity— II. Porphyry: 'Against Christians,'" *Expository Times* XLIII (Nov., 1931), pp. 72 – 78; and the exhaustive studies of Harnack.

easily be understood how that outstanding wisdom and admirable character, in which the entire life of Moses shines, can be harmonized with such a wicked imposture, or in what way he would have been able to think through that marvelous law, from which whatever good others possess has been borrowed, which provides for the glory of the one God and the holiness of the people, to further his fraud and imposture. Further, if he were an impostor, it is surprising that he followed a path plainly contrary to his design, in which he could easily be convicted of falsification. For if the account which he gives of the origin of the world is false, nothing would have been easier than to demonstrate its falsity, because of the small number of generations which he records between Adam and the flood, and between the flood and the people's departure from Egypt, since in the time of Moses some who had seen Joseph could still be living, whose parents would have seen Shem, who, up to the hundredth year of his life could have associated with Methuselah, who survived to that time, and who himself had seen Adam; thus the truth or falsity of the matter could have been discovered without difficulty. (3) If Moses was an impostor, and wished to deceive the Israelites, he certainly hoped that the Israelites would believe his lies and deceptions, but how would he have been able to convince them of so many and such great signs as are said to have been given both in Egypt and in the desert, if nothing of the sort had happened? Especially in view of the fact that he wrote for people who would have been witnesses, by ear and eye, of the events, and he wrote concerning actions which were not performed many centuries earlier, but in that very time, not secretly and in some corner, and before a few witnesses who could easily have been corrupted, but openly and in public before the eyes of six hundred thousand men [Exod. 12:37], and their irreconcilable enemies, who would be able to describe him as a falsifier? Would he have been able to hope that there would be among the people no one who doubted these claims, or who would not inquire into the truth of what happened in Egypt? Is it believable that, out of so many people, whom he repeatedly described most bitterly as rebellious and ungovernable, and whom he often afflicted with the most painful punishments, striking with sudden death not simply hundreds, but thousands, and [performing] similar actions by which he could have most justly aroused their anger against him, there was not one who exposed his deceit and imposture, when all of them are seen complaining and rebelling so unfairly against him? Finally, if he engaged in imposture, he certainly took some gain from it, either honor or wealth, as he might have gained authority (*imperium*) for himself and his posterity, or sought praise for wisdom and heroic character (*virtus*); but both the facts themselves and the sincerity with which he so frankly confessed his own sin, and above all his failure to believe, sufficiently show how far Moses was from desire for riches or honor.

xx. But perhaps the Israelites, recognizing the falsity of the accounts which were given by Moses, joined in deceit and imposture, in order to secure the greater glory of the nation. But (1) who dares believe that they were so senseless as to agree that they would not resist in such a tremendous fraud by which they were subjected to the unbearable (ἀβαστακτῷ) yoke of a most burdensome law, if they were convinced that this law was simply the invention of Moses? Is it possible to assert, in any true fashion, that, of six hundred thousand men, all would agree in such deceit, so that not one was found who would set himself against such a plan? (2) So far from truth is it that they secured honor and praise among others by this action that, on the contrary, the hatred and scorn of all came upon them, rightly; for who would maintain that it advanced the honor of a nation to have its worst sins and grumblings exposed to the eyes of the world, so that they were shown as the most stiff-necked and ungrateful of mortals, and the very heavy penalties by which God punished their obstinacy and rebellion were recorded more than once? Who does not see that these facts show forever the honesty of the [Israelite] nation? In short, there is no reason why a people of such stiff neck and so fond of pleasure would so readily have sought subjection to a most burdensome law, one the least transgression of which was so severely avenged, unless they were convinced of the divine quality (*divinitas*) of the call of Moses, and of the truth of his words.

XXI. The conversion of the world and the success of the gospel is a most striking argument for its divine quality, for unless the apostles were men of God and imparted heavenly truth, it is beyond comprehension who could have accomplished this, since their teaching lacked all those supports by which every human teaching is made popular and spread abroad, and was attacked stubbornly by those forces by which any teaching can be resisted: the authority of elders, the consensus of popular opinion, the favor of princes, the eloquence of orators, the subtlety of philosophers, agreement with human customs and inclination. [This teaching] was spread by a few ignorant and weak men, who were altogether foreign not only to deceit in teaching, but also to the appearance of it. They were not helped by the support of eloquence, [were] educated in no skill of pleading, [were] scorned and despised. By persuasion alone, without any support from authority and public approval, without the aid of weapons, through a thousand deaths and hardships and in the shortest time, [this teaching] was so spread to almost every place that it had overcome all obstacles, and emerged victor over other religions that were well furnished with all these supports, so that entire nations and kings themselves had embraced it, without hope of reward, and indeed with the certain prospect of evils which were absurd to reason and unwelcome to the flesh, and which would seem to drive people away from it rather than attract them to it.

XXII. Certainty is of three kinds: (1) mathematical, (2) moral, and (3) theological. (1) Mathematical or metaphysical certainty consists of first principles known through nature and in themselves, and of conclusions demonstrated from such principles, such as "the whole is greater than any part," and "the same object cannot both exist (*esse*) and not exist at the same time." (2) Moral certainty[11] is found in matters which cannot be demonstrated but which nevertheless are commended to belief by such most probable evidences and arguments that no prudent person can doubt them. [In this class are the conclusions] that the *Aeneid* was written by Virgil, and Livy's history by Livy. Although, to be sure, the matter is not known through itself, yet it is so witnessed to by unchanging report that nobody who has any conception of history and literature can doubt it. (3) Theological certainty is found in matters which, although they cannot be demonstrated, nor known through themselves or by nature, and do not depend on most probable evidence and moral arguments, yet [depend on] arguments truly theological and divine, namely, divine revelation, which therefore produce not merely a moral and conjectural certainty, but a faith truly divine. Scripture does not hold (*habeo*) metaphysical certainty. If it did, the assent which we would give it would take the form of knowledge (*scientiam*), not faith. It does not hold a certainty simply moral and probable. If it did, our faith would be no more certain than the historical assent which

11. "Moral" here is not an ethical concept, except insofar as there is an ethical obligation to be bound by theoretical truth.

is given to human writings. But it does hold a theological and infallible certainty, which cannot deceive the person who is faithful and illuminated by the Spirit of God.

XXIII. The prophets made no mistakes when they wrote inspired by God and as prophets, not even in matters of little significance, because if they did, faith in the whole of Scripture would be turned into doubt. But in other ways, as men, they were capable of error. In this way, David erred in the letter concerning the killing of Uriah [II Sam. 11:14 – 15], which has historical but not normative authority, and Nathan erred in the advice which, without seeking God's will, he gave David about building the temple (II Sam. 7:3), because the influence of the Holy Spirit was neither universal nor continuous, nor is it to be understood as a normal motion or effect of nature (II Kings 2:17).

XXIV. The apostles were infallible in faith, not in morals, and the Spirit was their guide in all truth so that they never erred, but not in all godly living (*pietas*) so that they never sinned, because they were like us in all things. The pretense and hypocrisy of Peter, recorded in Galatians 2:12, was a sin in life, not an error in faith, a moral lapse and failure in conduct resulting from weakness and fear of incurring the hatred of the Jews. It was not, however, an intellectual error (*error mentis*) resulting from ignorance of Christian freedom, his understanding of which is sufficiently shown by his fellowship with Gentiles previous to the arrival of the Jews.

XXV. When Paul says, "I say, not the Lord" (I Cor. 7:10[12]), he does not deny the inspiration of the Lord, by whose words he vindicates his own (v. 40). Rather this precept, or law expressly given by the Lord, was hidden before him, so that the meaning is that this controversy over sinful desertion had not yet arisen in Christ's time, nor had he had any opportunity of settling it, which Paul, illumined by the Spirit, now did.

XXVI. Anything in the Law which seems absurd and useless will be found by the pious and wise to be of the greatest significance for the motivating of obedience, the overthrowing of idolatry, the cultivation of morals, and the proclamation of the Messiah, if taken rightly and properly. The genealogies, and other records that seem unnecessary, are witnesses to the origin, spread, and preservation of the church and to the fulfillment of the promises of a Messiah descended from the seed of Abraham and David.

XXVII. The prophecy of Hosea (Hos. 1:2) does not command that he marry the adulteress, for the sons of a marriage cannot be called illegitimate, which is the meaning of this verse. But this must be understood as allegory, since Israel, impure because of her idolatry, is represented by this symbol.

Apparent Contradictions in Scripture

QUESTION **5**

Are there in Scripture true contradictions, or any irreconcilable passages, which cannot be resolved or harmonized in any way? (Negative)

I. When the divine quality of Scripture, which was argued in the preceding question, has been accepted, its infallibility follows of necessity.[1] But in every age the enemies of true religion and of Scripture have thought that they had found contradictory passages in Scripture, and have vigorously presented them in order to overthrow its authority; for example, Porphyry, Lucian, and Julian the Apostate among the pagans of antiquity, and today various atheists, who in hostile fashion declare that there are contradictions and irreconcilable differences which cannot be harmonized in any way. Therefore this particular question must be discussed with them, so that the integrity of Scripture may be upheld against their impiety by a completed fabric and covering.

II. Our controversy is not with open atheists and pagans, who do not recognize Holy Scripture, but with others who, although they seem to accept it, yet indirectly deny it in this manner: for example, the enthusiasts, who allege the

---

1. The *divinitas* of Scripture means that it fully shares the great divine quality of unqualified truthfulness.

imperfection of the written word in order to attract people to their esoteric word or special revelations; the Roman Catholics, who, although they defend the divine quality of Scripture against the atheist, yet do not fear to oppose, with powerful weapons, and to the full extent of their ability, their own cause and that of all Christendom, and to enter the struggle as its enemies, by teaching the corruption of the sources,[2] in order to win agreement for the authority of their Vulgate version; and finally, various libertines, who, although living in the bosom of the church, never stop calling attention to some "irreconcilable differences" and "contradictions," so as to erode the authority of Scripture.[3]

III. To deal with them, the scholars (*doctores*) follow various paths. Some think the question may be easily handled by granting that the sacred writers could have made mistakes, by failure of memory, or in unimportant details. This argument is used by Socinus when he treats the authority of Scripture, by Castellio in his *Dialogue*, and by others. But this does not counter the argument of the atheists; it joins them in a blasphemous manner. Others hold that the Hebrew and Greek sources have been corrupted in places, through the malice of Jews and heretics, but that the correction is easy by means of the Vulgate and the infallible authority of the church. This is the teaching of most Roman Catholics. We will argue against it in a later section,[4] when we discuss the purity of the sources. Others concede that small errors have appeared in Scripture, and remain, which cannot be corrected by reliance on any

---

2. *Fontes* ("sources") is Turretin's regular word for the Hebrew and Greek texts of the Bible. A Renaissance interest has become basic in his orthodoxy.

3. *Enthusiastae* (believers in special revelations) and *libertini* (rejecters of authority) were familiar opponents of orthodox Protestantism within its fold, ever since the early days of the Reformation.

4. See locus 2, question 10, below.

manuscript or by collation, but which are not to be ascribed to the sacred writers, but explained partly by the ravages of time and partly by the faults of copyists and editors, and which do not destroy the authority of Scripture because they occur only with regard to unnecessary or unimportant statements. Scaliger, Cappel, Amama, Voss, and others are of this opinion. Finally, others uphold the integrity of Scripture and do not deny that various seeming contradictions—not, however, true or real ones—occur; [they believe] that these passages are difficult to understand but not altogether contradictory and impossible. This is the more common opinion of the orthodox, which we follow as the more safe and the more true.

IV. It is not a question of errors in spelling and punctuation, or of variant readings, which everyone admits are not infrequent, nor whether the copies that we have agree so completely with the original autographs that they do not differ in the least. But the question is whether our manuscripts so differ from the originals that the true meaning has been corrupted, and the original texts can no longer be regarded as the rule of faith and practice.

V. It is not a question of the faultiness of some individual codices, or of the errors which the carelessness of copyists and printers may have introduced into the copies of this or that edition. No one denies that there are various corruptions of this sort. The question is whether there are corruptions and "universal errors" so distributed through all the copies, whether handwritten or printed, that they cannot be corrected either by the comparison of variant readings or from Scripture itself and the collating of parallel passages, and whether these are true and real contradictions, which we deny, or merely apparent ones.

VI. The reasons are: (1) Scripture is "God-breathed" (II Tim. 3:16). The Word of God cannot lie (Ps. 19:8 – 9; Heb. 6:18), it cannot perish and pass away (Matt. 5:18), it abides forever (I Peter 1:25), and it is truth itself (John 17:17). How could this be predicated of it if there were deadly contradictions, and if God had allowed the sacred writers either to err and to forget, or to introduce into it irreparable deceit?

VII. (2) Unless unimpaired integrity is attributed to Scripture, it cannot be regarded as the sole rule of faith and practice, and a wide door is opened to atheists, libertines, enthusiasts, and others of that sort of profane people to undermine its authority and overthrow the foundation of salvation. Since error cannot be part of the faith, how can a Scripture which is weakened by contradictions and corruptions be regarded as authentic and divine? Nor should it be said that these corruptions are only in matters of little significance, which do not affect the fundamentals of the faith. For as soon as the authenticity of Scripture has been found wanting, even if it be a single corruption [of the text] that cannot be corrected, how can our faith any longer be sustained? If corruption is conceded in matters of little importance, why not also in others of more significance? Who will be able to give me faith that there has been no forgetfulness or deceit in the fundamental passages? What answer can be given the subtle atheist or heretic who persistently claims that this or that text, unfavorable to him, rests on falsehood? The reply should not be that divine providence has willed the [Scripture] be preserved from serious corruptions, but not from minor ones. For not only is this an arbitrary assumption, but it also cannot be made without grave insult [to Scripture], implying that it lacks something necessary for its full self-authentication, nor can it easily be believed that God, who spoke and inspired every single word to God-inspired men, would not have provided for the preservation of all. If human beings preserve their words with the greatest care so that they will not be changed or corrupted, especially when—as is the case, for instance, with wills and contracts—they are of some importance, how much more should God be thought to have taken care for his Word, which he willed to have the status of testament and public notice of his covenant with us, so that nothing could corrupt it, especially when he could have easily foreseen and prevented such corruptions, to uphold the faith of his church?

VIII. There are four main arguments for the integrity of Scripture, and the purity of the sources. (1) Above all, the providence of God, who, since he wished to provide for our faith, could be expected to keep the Scripture pure and uncontaminated, both by inspiring the sacred authors who wrote it, and by protecting it from the efforts of enemies who left nothing untried to destroy it, that our faith might always have a firm point on which to rest. (2) The religion of the Jews, who were always careful guardians of the accuracy of the sacred codices, even to the point of superstition. (3) The diligence of the Masoretes, who, by their marks, placed, as it were, a fence around the Law. (4) The number and completeness of copies, with the result that even if one codex could have been corrupted, all could not be.

IX. Whatever contradictions seem to be in Scripture are apparent but not real. [They appear] only with respect to the understanding of us who are not able to perceive and grasp everywhere their harmony. They are not in the material itself. If the laws of true contradiction are observed, so that seeming contradictions are brought together in accordance with simple identity of qualities (*secundum idem*), circumstance (*ad idem*), or time, the various so-called contradictions of Scripture can readily be reconciled, for either (1) they are simply not discussions of the same things, as when James ascribes justification to works, although Paul disparages them. One speaks of an explanatory justification of effect, *a posteriori*; the other of a justification of cause, *a priori*. So also in Luke 6:36 mercy is required, "be merciful," while it is forbidden in Deuteronomy 19:13, "you shall show no mercy." One commandment is for private citizens; one for magistrates. Or (2) the same thing is not described according to the same qualities, as Matthew in 26:11 denies the presence of Christ in the world, "You will not always have me," while in 28:20 he promises it, "I am with you always, to the end of time." One statement is made with respect to the human nature [of Christ] and his bodily presence; the other with respect to the divine nature and his spiritual presence. Or (3) the statements are not made with regard to the same circumstances, as when one is absolute and the other relative. "Honor your father," but, Luke 14:26, "if anyone does not hate his father." One statement is to be understood as absolute; the other as relative, in that our [earthly] father must be loved less and placed after Christ. Or the statements do not refer to the same time, whence the maxim, "Distinguish the scriptural times and relationships." Thus circumcision is both exalted, as the great privilege of the Jews (Rom. 3:1 — 2), and deprecated as a thing of naught (Gal. 5:3). One statement refers to the time of the Old Testament, when it was the ordinary sacrament and seal of the righteousness of faith; the other to the time of the gospel after the abrogation of the ceremonial law. Likewise the apostles were sent on a special mission to the Jews alone before Christ's passion, and were forbidden to go to the Gentiles, "Do not go into the way of the Gentiles" (Matt. 10:5), but after the resurrection [they were sent] on a general mission to all people (Mark 16:15).[5]

x. Although we attribute absolute integrity to Scripture, we do not hold that the copyists and printers have been inspired, but only that the providence of God has so

5. The "longer ending" of Mark, assumed by Turretin's age to be authentic.

watched over the copyists that, although many errors could
have entered, they did not, or at least they did not enter
the codices in such a manner that they cannot easily be
corrected by comparison with other copies (ex *collatione
aliorum*) or with [other parts of] Scripture itself.[6] So the
basis of the purity and integrity of the sources does not
rest on the inerrancy of human beings but on the providence of God, who, although the men who copied the
sacred works could have introduced many errors, always
carefully looked after them and corrected them, or else
they can easily be corrected either by comparison with the
Scripture itself or with better codices. Therefore it was not
necessary to make all the scribes infallible, but only so to
guide them that the true reading can always be found, and
this book far surpasses all others whatsoever in purity.

XI. Although we cannot quickly find an obvious harmo-
nization, free from all obscurities, between Scripture texts
which involve names, numbers, or dates, these problems
are not to be quickly classed as insoluble, or if they are
called insoluble, they are such because of human ignorance, and not because of the problem itself, so that it is
better to acknowledge our ignorance than to accept any
contradiction. These records are not written so exactly that
all the circumstances were included. Many facts were certainly condensed into an epitome; others, which seemed
unnecessary, were omitted; and it is even possible that
these passages have various relationships which were well
known to the writers, although now hidden from us.
Hence Peter Martyr says very well concerning II Kings 8:17,
"Granted that there are obscure passages in the chrono-
logies, it is not to be conceded that, for the purpose of
reconciling them, we say that the sacred codex is false. For
God, who in his mercy willed that the holy (*divinus*) books

---

6. It will be noted that the study of text criticism is required by this theology.

be preserved for us, gave them whole and not corrupted. Therefore when we are not able to explain the number of years, the ignorance under which we work must be admitted, and it must be remembered that the sacred book is written with such brevity that it is not easy to find out from what point the reckoning of time was begun; the Scripture, which, if it failed in one or another place, would also be suspect in others, remains uncorrupted." And again, about I Kings 15:1 [he says], "It is not uncommon, in this record, for the number of years which is attributed to the kings to appear to have little consistency. Doubts of this kind can be dispelled on manifold grounds. It may be that one and the same year is attributed to two persons, when it was not lived through its entirety by either. Sometimes sons ruled jointly with their parents for some years, and these years were assigned now to the reign of the parents, and now to that of the children. An interregnum sometimes took place and the empty period was attributed, now to the earlier king, and now to the later. There are even some years, in which the sovereigns ruled illegally and without religious sanction (*tyrannice et impie*), which are therefore disregarded, and not added to the other years of the reign."

XII. Luke 3:36, concerning the younger Cain who is placed between Arpachshad and Shelah, contrary to the truth of the Mosaic record (Gen. 11:13), offers indeed a difficult problem, which learned scholars interpret in different ways, but it should not be regarded as an insoluble one, since various forms of solution are possible. For our part, not mentioning other opinions, we consider most appropriate that which regards this Cain as a suppositious and spurious [person], who crept in, through the carelessness of copyists, from the Septuagint version, in which he had existed before the time of Christ, as the chronology of Demetrius quoted in Eusebius's *De praeperatione evangelii* witnesses; or through some pious intent [of copyists], who did not want to oppose Luke to the Septuagint, whose authority was then considerable. The following data support this: (1) the authority of Moses and of the Books of Chronicles, which make no mention of him in their genealogies, in which there are three places where clearly he should have been included (Gen. 10:24 and 11:13; I Chron. 1:18). (2) The Chaldean paraphrase, which altogether omits this Cain both in Genesis and in Chronicles. (3) Josephus does not mention him, nor does Berosus to whom he refers, nor [Julius] Africanus whom Eusebius quotes. (4) [If his existence is upheld] the sacred chronology would be confused, and the Mosaic record would be brought into doubt, if Cain is inserted between Arpachshad and Shelah, and Noah becomes the eleventh after Abraham, not the tenth as Moses states. (5)[This Cain] is not found in all the codices. Our Beza witnesses to his absence from his oldest manuscript, and Ussher states (*Dissertatio de Cainane*, p. 196) that he has seen a copy of Luke in Greek and Latin on a very old parchment, in large letters without breathings and accents, which was long ago taken from Greece to France and placed in the monastery of Saint Irenaeus near Lyons, and in 1562 removed, and then taken to England and given to Cambridge University, in which Cain in not listed.[7] Scaliger affirms, in his prologue to the chronicle of Eusebius, that this Cain is lacking in the oldest copies of Luke. Whatever may be the facts, although this passage in Luke may be said to contain an error, Luke's authenticity cannot be brought into doubt on account of it, for (1) the corruption is not universal; (2) little falsehood is contained in it, and the correction for that is easily supplied from Moses, so that there was no

---

7. The manuscript now known as Codex Bezae Cantabrigiensis (D).

need for the learned Isaac Voss to be concerned over the purity of the Hebrew codices, that he might defend the authenticity of the Septuagint.[8]

XIII. If there is a great difference in the genealogies of Christ which are recorded by Matthew and Luke, both as to the persons and the number of persons, this ought not to seem remarkable, because they do not record the same matters, but different ones. Matthew gives the genealogy of Joseph, whose family derives from David through Solomon. Luke traces the family of Mary to this same David through another son, Nathan. Matthew, after the Hebrew custom, included the wife's family in the husband's; Luke, however, wished to supply what had been omitted, by reporting Mary's family tree, so that the genealogy of Christ would stand out, so to speak, full and complete, from both parents, so that there would be no place for the doubts of the weak or the scoffing of the enemies of the gospel, and that the former would be upheld, and the latter won over, to the conviction that according to the predictions of the prophets Christ was the true and natural son of David, whether reference was made to her husband Joseph, into whose family Mary passed by marriage, or to Mary herself. It is most certain that heiresses (*virgines;* ἐπικλήρους), such as the blessed virgin was, who received a dowry from the family inheritance, could not marry outside their own tribe and family. Luke's genealogy also, therefore, refers to Joseph, not to Mary, for it was not customary to prepare a genealogy through the women, for they were listed either with their parents and brothers if they were unmarried, or with their husbands if they were espoused; hence the maxim of the Jews, "the mother's family is not the family."

XIV. Although the father of Joseph is called Jacob by Matthew, and Heli by Luke (Matt. 1:16; Luke 3:23), there is no

8. Nestle brackets τοῦ καϊνάν in this verse.

contradiction, because this is to be understood as of two different matters (κατ' ἄλλα καὶ ἄλλο). First, it is not absurd for one son to have two fathers in different senses, when one is the natural father who begat the son from himself, and the other the legal father who adopted him to himself from another family by full process of law. In this way Manasseh and Ephraim were natural sons of Joseph but legal sons of Jacob by adoptions; and Obed the grandfather of David had one natural father, Boaz, but also a legal one, Mahlon, the former husband of his mother Ruth, to whom Boaz the second husband raised seed according to the law. Thus Jacob was the natural father of Joseph, but Heli may be called the father of Joseph. This may be either in a legal sense, as [Julius] Africanus supposed, because on the death of Heli without children, Jacob had married his wife according to the law (Deut. 25:5) and fathered Joseph, Mary's husband, from her. Or it may be that Heli was the natural father of Mary and thus in a civil sense the father of Joseph by reason of the marriage contracted by his daughter, through which he became a father [-in-law], in which sense Naomi speaks of her daughters-in-law as her daughters (Ruth 1:11 − 12), which manner of speaking is in use among all people.[9] Or it may be said that not Joseph, but Christ, is son of Heli, the phrase "as was supposed" being indeed parenthetical, not meaning, however, as commonly read, "being, as was supposed, the son of Joseph," but rather, "Jesus, who was supposed to be the son of Joseph, being the son of Heli," that is, his grandson, through the Virgin Mary, nor is it improper to pass in this manner from grandfather to grandson, especially if the fathers have died, and all the more in this

9. The distinction between "legal" and "civil" is theological. "Legal" refers to the covenant law, "civil" to "secular" arrangements, including those within the covenant community.

case, because Christ was without father according to his human nature... .[10]

XXII. In II Samuel 24:24 David is said to buy a threshing floor and oxen from Araunah for 50 shekels of silver. In I Chronicles 21:25 reference is made to 600 shekels of gold. A reconciliation is easy from the nature of the transaction: he gave 50 shekels for the part in which he first built an altar, but after he learned, through a heavenly fire that came down, that this was the place God had chosen for the temple, then, not satisfied with the small area, he bought the whole field, and the hill, for 600 shekels... .

XXXIV. When Christ forbids swearing "at all" (Matt. 5:34), he does not intend to condemn the oath absolutely and simply, for elsewhere it is allowed and approved, and it is required by God (Exod. 22:8, 10 – 11; Lev. 5:4; Num. 5:19 – 20; Prov. 18:18; Heb. 6:16), but rather certain forms of oath which were used by the Jews, and which are mentioned in the same place, namely, those by heaven, earth, Jerusalem, the head and other created things of that nature, all of which are condemned by Christ as rash and forbidden. In this way universal terms often are restricted to some particular (*ad certam speciam*), [for example] John 10:8: "All who came before me are thieves"; all, that is, who were not called or sent, or who said that they themselves or some other was the shepherd of the sheep. And I Corinthians 10:23, "All things are lawful to me,'" and 9:22, "I have become all things to all"; that is, in matters that are

10. I have not translated paragraphs 15 – 21, 23 – 33, and 35, more than eight pages in the Edinburgh edition. They are not necessary for the theological argument, are by no means an exhaustive list of seeming contradictions in Scripture, and deal mainly with factual problems that have received adequate attention from later commentators in the light of later research in philology, archaeology, and other disciplines. What is translated illustrates Turretin's method, which gives theological problems, as in paragraph 34 below, and genealogical ones the same theoretical significance.

lawful and indifferent. Evil and sinful acts are not lawful to anyone. . . .

XXXVI. From the above it is clear that the various difficult passages which are used to deny the authority of Scripture, which we have illustrated, are not irreconcilable contradictions, although they are indeed difficulties. There are also many others which the Roman Catholics use to argue the corruption of the sources by Jews and heretics, but they will be better dealt with later, when we discuss the authoritative version.[11]

11. Questions 11 and 12, below.

The Knowledge of Scriptural Authority

QUESTION **6**

How does the authority of Holy (*divinus*) Scripture become known to us? Does it, either in itself or on our part, depend upon the witness of the church? (Negative, against the Roman Catholics)

I. The purpose of the Roman Catholics, in this and other controversies which they maintain over the Scripture, is not obscure, namely, to reject the judgment of Scripture, in which they cannot find enough sanction to protect their errors, and to appeal to the church, that is, to their pope, and so become judges of their own case. Thus, when formerly doctrine was debated on the basis of its agreement or nonagreement with Scripture, now debate has begun on Scripture itself—whether it is proper for religious controversies to be settled by its authority and witness. A severe struggle has been carried on concerning its origin, necessity, perfection, and perspicuity, for the purpose of diminishing them [Scripture's authority and witness], if not completely rejecting them. Quite properly what Irenaeus said of the heretics of his day may be applied to them [Roman Catholics]: "When opposed by Scriptures they became opponents of the Scriptures, as if they were incorrect or without authority."

II. It must be noted that some of them go to extremes and some speak more moderately in this matter. Some indeed simply deny the authority of Scripture, in itself and apart from the church, and hold it to be no more worthy of faith (I shudder to say it) than the Qur'an or the works of Livy or Aesop. Those who began to dispute the authority of Scripture with our [theologians] in the past century uttered this blasphemy. Of this the impious words of Hosius, in his work against Brent, are an example, when he declares that it is possible to assert in a reverent sense "the Scriptures have only the weight of Aesop's fables if they are deprived of the authority of the Church," and Eck declared, "Scripture is not authoritative except by the authority of the church...."[1] Because it seemed to others that this blasphemy had been rightly attacked by our [theologians], they spoke more carefully, expressing their teaching in such a way as to admit that absolutely and in itself Scripture is authoritative and of divine quality, since it comes from God the source of all truth, but they hold that relative to us its authority exists only on the witness of the church, through whose ministry it becomes known to us and is understood as of divine quality. From this arose the distinction between authority as to its nature (*quoad se*) and as to our understanding (*quoad nos*), which Bellarmine, Stapleton, and others have since brought forward.

III. But however they present their teaching, if we think of the matter correctly, it will be obvious that this distinction results in confusion, and hides the evil of an impious doctrine, rather than clarifying the truth of the matter. For since the authority is that of communicators and relationships, it cannot be understood absolutely, but relatively;

1. Further quotations from sixteenth-century writers have been omitted from the translation. They may or may not be in context, but they add nothing of theological import to what is given. In any case, they represent an early stage of anti-Protestant polemic that Turretin realizes does not represent the real issue.

therefore, Scripture cannot be authoritative in itself unless it is so also to our understanding,[2] for whatever arguments demonstrate its authority in itself ought also to move us to agreement, so that it will be authoritative to our understanding. If the authority of Scripture for our understanding depends on the witness of the church, as if that were the formal ground on account of which I believe that it has a divine quality (*esse divinam*), then of necessity its authority in itself depends [on such witness], which some admit fully. Nor is any other teaching easily derived from the other controversies that they keep up, for how can they deny the perfection, perspicuity, or purity [of Scripture] if they believe it to be truly of divine origin (*authenticus*)?

IV. That the state of the question may be clear: (1) It is not a question of whether the Holy Scriptures are authentic and of divine quality; this our adversaries do not deny, or at least they want to seem to believe it. But [the question is] how are they known to us to be of such quality, or by what argument can this divine quality (*divinitas*) be demonstrated for us? The Roman Catholics make it depend on the witness of the church, and want the chief cause by which we are moved to believe the authenticity of Scripture to be the voice of the church. On the other hand, although we do not deny that the witness of the church has its value, as will appear later, yet we maintain that primarily and essentially Scripture is to be believed by us of divine quality on account of itself, or of the marks imprinted upon it, not on account of the church.

V. (2) It is not a question of the principle, or efficient cause, of faith by which we believe the divine quality of Scripture, that is, of whether or not the Holy Spirit produces it in us. This belongs to another question concern-

2. Revelation is complete and meaningful only when it has been received.

ing the freedom of the will,[3] and adversaries, such as Stapleton and Cano, agree with us. But here the question is about the argument or chief means which that Spirit uses to convince us of this truth; is it a direct (*inartificialis*) witness of the church, as the Roman Catholics hold, or a rational (*artificialis*) one based on marks (*notae*) in Scripture itself, as we maintain?[4]

VI. Just as it is possible to speak of a threefold cause of the manifestation of anything—objective, efficient, and instrumental—so a threefold question can be framed about the recognition of the divine quality of Scripture: first, the argument on account of which I believe; second, the principle, or efficient cause, by which I am led to belief; third, the means and instrument through which I believe. The threefold question is answered in a threefold manner. Scripture, in its marks, becomes the form of argument on account of which I believe; the Holy Spirit becomes the means or the efficient cause and principle by which I am made to believe; the church is the instrument and means through which I believe. So if it is asked why or on account of what I believe Scripture to be of divine quality, I will reply that this happens through Scripture itself which proves itself to be such by its marks. If it is asked how or by what it happens that I believe, I will reply, by the Holy Spirit, who produces this faith within me. Finally, if it is asked by what means or organ I believe this, I will reply, through the church, which God uses in giving me Scripture.

VII. (3) There is no question concerning the means whose

3. The question of the will is discussed by Turretin largely in locus 4, *De decretis Dei*, translated in Beardslee, *Reformed Dogmatics* (Grand Rapids: Baker, 1977), pp. 337 – 359, and in locus 10, *De libero hominis arbitrio in statu peccati*.

4. This appeal to reason rather than to authority was a natural development in Protestantism, which had rejected the "external" authority of the church.

service the Holy Spirit uses in convincing us of the authority of Scripture; we readily grant that this is the church. But the question concerns the primary argument and cause whereby we are led to faith, not human but God-based (*divinus*), which they [Roman Catholics] place in the church; we believe it is not to be sought outside Scripture itself.

VIII. (4) There is no question that divine revelation is absolutely and simply the formal ground of our faith. Our adversaries acknowledge this with us. But what is that first and clearest revelation which ought to be accepted by us through and on account of itself, not on account of anything else which is better known to us, and which is therefore the most universal and primary basis of faith through which all ought to be proved but which itself [is proved by] nothing beyond it: is such revelation to be sought in Scripture or in the church? We hold that such revelation is found only in the Scripture, which is the first and infallible rule of faith. The Roman Catholics maintain that it is to be sought in the word and witness of the church. Stapleton says, in his book *On the Authority of the Church Against Whittaker*, book 1: "The supreme external witness on earth is the voice of the church" (chap. 8), and, "God, when he speaks by the church, does not speak in any other manner than if he were speaking in visions and dreams, or in whatever other form of supernatural revelation God may have spoken through" (chap. 9), and "The entire formal ground of our faith is God revealing through the church" (chap. 14). . . .[5]

IX. The question is therefore reduced to these terms: Why or on account of what do we believe Scripture to be the Word of God? or, what argument does the Holy Spirit

5. Other quotations which embody the same thought have been omitted from the translation.

use primarily to convince us of the divine quality of Scripture? Is it the witness or voice of the church, or the marks and criteria imprinted in Scripture itself? Our adversaries assert the former, we the latter.

x. That the authority of Scripture does not depend, either in itself or with regard to our understanding, on the witness of the church, is proved (1) because the church is founded on Scripture (Eph. 2:20), and all its authority is received from Scripture. This our adversaries cannot deny, since, when the question is raised they can go nowhere but to Scripture for an answer. Therefore [the church] cannot produce the authority of Scripture either in itself or with regard to our understanding, unless we maintain that the cause depends on the effect, the beginning on that which has been begun, and the foundation on the superstructure. Nor should it be objected that both conclusions can be true; the church receives its authority from Scripture, and Scripture in turn from the church, as John [the Baptist] bore witness to Christ, who gave witness to John. For it is one thing to give witness to another as a servant, in which way John is a witness to Christ—one through whom the Jews might believe (John 1:7), but not on account of whom. It is quite another matter to offer authority as a lord, which Christ did toward John. (2) [If Roman Catholic doctrine were true] the authority of the church would be prior to that of Scripture and so the primary matter of belief, on which from the first our faith would depend and into which it would ultimately be resolved, [a doctrine] which our adversaries do not accept, for they wish the authority of the church to depend on Scripture. (3) Obviously it is to argue in a circle when the authority of the church is proved by Scripture and then the authority of Scripture by the church. (4) Our adversaries have never agreed on what is to be understood by the church—whether it is the contemporary church or that of antiquity, the whole church or its representatives,[6] particular or universal; or what will be the act that witnesses to the authority of Scripture—whether it is certified [at a given time] by some judicial decision, or made effective through a continual and unbroken tradition. (5) A fallible and human witness, such as that of the church, cannot establish supernatural faith (*fides divina*). Nor, if God does speak through the church today, does it follow that the church is infallible, because special and extraordinary inspiration, such as kept apostles and prophets free from error, and of which Christ spoke strictly when he said that the Holy Spirit would lead the apostles into all truth (John 16:14 [13]) is one thing, but common and ordinary [inspiration] is another,[7] which does not produce [apostolically] inspired pastors.

XI. That Scripture becomes known to us through itself is proved (1) by the nature of Scripture. For just as the law does not receive its authority from the lower judges who interpret it, nor from the heralds who proclaim it, but only from the prince who establishes it, and as a will obtains its weight from the wishes of the testators, not from the notary by whom it is drawn, and as a measuring rod (*regula*) determines measurement because of its own perfection, not because of the workman who uses it, so Scripture, which is the law of the highest prince, the will of the heavenly Father, and the undeviating rule of faith, cannot hold its authority over us from the church, but only from itself. (2) [By] the nature of final categories and first principles. For as these are known of themselves and are undemonstrated [principles] which cannot be proved from any others, which would lead to an infinite regression—

6. *Ecclesia repraesentiva* (i.e., a council, or the pope and cardinals, or similar body).

7. Turretin here makes an important theological distinction, which later theologians described as the difference between inspiration and illumination.

"it is necessary that the beginning of every branch of knowledge be what cannot be investigated," says Basil—so Scripture, which is the first principle in the supernatural order, is known by itself, and there is no way in which it can be demonstrated and made known to us by arguments sought outside it. If God placed marks in all the principles by which they may be known by all, there can be no doubt that he placed such in this sacred principle which is supremely necessary for salvation. (3) By analogy. As sense objects are recognized and known without any other external argument, from the inner relationship and the inclination of the faculty to the object, provided that the faculties of sensation are healthy—light by its own splendor, food by its own flavor, odor by its fragrance, are immediately recognized by us even in the absence of a witness—so the Scripture, which with respect to the new creation is described for us in a spiritual sense by the symbol of glorious light (Ps. 119:105), delightful food (Ps. 19:10; Isa. 55:1 – 2; Heb. 5:14), and most fragrant perfume (Song of Sol. 1:3), is easily recognized through itself by the senses of the new man and shows itself to them, and demonstrates itself by its own light, pleasantness, and fragrance, so that there is no need to seek elsewhere for what this light, food, and perfume teach that they are. (4) By the testimony of adversaries [Roman Catholics], who demonstrate the divine quality of Scripture by its marks. Bellarmine says, "As to the Holy Scriptures, which are contained in the writings of prophets and apostles, nothing is more knowable or more certain, so that it must be a most stupid act to fail to have faith in them" (*De Verbo Dei* 1.2)....[8]

XII. We do not deny that many functions of the church with respect to Scripture are proper. (1) That it be a guard-

8. Quotations from other Roman Catholic sources of similar import have been omitted from the translation.

ian of the oracles of God, which were entrusted to it, who protects the authentic record of the covenant of grace with the highest fidelity, like a notary (Rom. 3:2). (2) A guide which points to the Scripture, and leads toward it. (3) A defender (*vindex*) who protects and vindicates it by distinguishing the genuine books from the corrupted, in which sense the church is called Scripture's bulwark (I Tim. 3:16 [15]). (4) A herald, who preaches and proclaims it (II Cor. 5:19; Rom. 10:16). (5) An interpreter who investigates and makes plain its true meaning. But these functions are all ministerial, not magisterial, so that indeed we believe through the church but not on account of the church, as those who believed in Christ believed through John the Baptist, not on account of him (John 1:7), and Christ became known to the Samaritans through the Samaritan woman, not on account of her (John 4:39).

XIII. The formation of faith, considered objectively with regard to the facts to be believed, is one thing, and another when considered subjectively with regard to the act of believing. The first is in Scripture and the external witness of the Holy Spirit expressed in Scripture; the second in the Spirit's internal witness impressed on the conscience[9] and speaking in the heart. Since both the setting forth of truth in the Word and its application in the heart are necessary for the engendering of faith, the Holy Spirit operates in both, in the Word and in the heart. Therefore he is properly said to witness in the Word, objectively, by means of the argument on account of which we believe. Also, less properly, he is said to witness in the heart efficiently, through the means of the principle in virtue of which we believe, in which sense the Spirit who presents internal witness of the divinity of Christ and the truth of gospel is said to

9. "Conscience" in Turretin's usage is a universal self-knowledge before God—part of human nature and more than a simple sense of right and wrong.

"witness, because the Spirit is truth" (I John 5:6 [7]); that is, the Spirit, acting in the hearts of the faithful, witnesses that the teaching of the gospel handed down by the Spirit is true and of divine quality.[10]

XIV. When the French Confession says (article 5), "We believe the books of Scripture to be canonical, not so much by the common consent of the church as by the witness and internal urging of the Holy Spirit,"[11] by "Holy Spirit" must be understood the Spirit speaking both in the Word and in the heart. So the same Spirit, acting objectively in the Word to set forth the truth, acts also efficiently in the heart to impress this truth on our minds, and so is very different from fanatical enthusiasm (*Spiritus Enthusiasticus*).

XV. A personal decision of the Spirit, which is such with regard to the person (*subjectus*) whose it is, is one thing; but a personal decision which is such in terms of its origin (*originaliter*), because it depends on the individual will of a human being, is another. We grant that the first is involved here, but not the second, because the Spirit that witnesses in us concerning the divine quality of Scripture is not limited to individuals with regard to his principle of operation and origin, but is common to the whole church, and to all believers in whom he has engendered the same faith, although he is such subjectively in regard to each individual, because given personally to individual believers.

XVI. Although the church, considered formally and in

10. It will be noted that, formally, Turretin's pneumatology is well thought out and pervades his doctrine; it is intended to control divisive claims to special revelation rather than to encourage experiments in freedom.

11. This is Turretin's text, agreeing in substance with Article 4 of the Toulouse edition of 1864. See Philip Schaff, *Creeds of Christendom* (New York: Harper and Brothers, 1877; reprint ed., Grand Rapids: Baker Book House, 1977), vol. 3, p. 361; B. A. Gerrish, *The Faith of Christendom* (Cleveland: World Publishing Co., 1963), p. 151; Arthur C. Cochrane, *Reformed Confessions of the Sixteenth Century* (Philadelphia: Westminster, 1966), p. 145.

connection with the act of writing, is older than Scripture, it cannot be called such materially and with respect to the substance of teaching, because the Word of God is older than this church, since it is its foundation and seed. (1) The dispute is not over the witness of the church of the ancient patriarchs who lived before the Scripture, but of the contemporary church, which is much more recent.

XVII. Although believers are convinced of the divine quality of Scripture by the witness of the Holy Spirit, it does not follow that all who have this Spirit should agree in accepting particular books equally, because, since he is not given to all in the same measure, so neither does he endow all with the light of equal knowledge either with regard to the essential (*principium*) of religion or of its dogmas, or move them to consent with equal effectiveness. Therefore some Protestants have been able to doubt the canonicity of one or another canonical book, because they were not yet sufficiently illumined by the light of the Holy Spirit.

XVIII. It is not always necessary for one thing to be proved by another. Some matters are self-evident, according to the philosophers, like the ultimate categories of things and final distinctions and first principles, which cannot be externally demonstrated but are evident in their own light, and so are presupposed as certain and not to be doubted, and if anyone does question them, he is not to be answered with arguments, but delivered to those responsible for him or coerced by punishments, as one who by the testimony of the philosopher[12] lacks either reason or discipline. Thus in the *Posterior Analytics* he says that anything is axiomatic which has no external cause for its truth, "which must both exist and be known by itself"; that is, which is not only self-evident, but which also simply can-

---

12. "Philosopher" here is singular, a retention of the old usage by which Aristotle is so designated, as the context shows. In the first part of the sentence "philosophers" was plural.

not be honestly denied by anyone whose reason is sound. Since Scripture is a first principle, and primary and infallible truth, what is strange in proving it by itself? (2) Scripture can prove itself, either a part proving the rest, as when we debate with Jews on the basis of the Old Testament, or the whole proving the whole, not by a direct argument of witness, but by a rational and logical one, because in it are found the divine marks which are not present in the writings of humans. This is not special pleading, for these criteria are separate from Scripture, not materially but formally, as adjuncts and properties which can be demonstrated with regard to the subject; nor is it a demonstration of an unknown through something equally unknown, because the marks are better known to us, just as we demonstrate a cause by its effects, and a subject by its properties. (3) The argument of the Roman Catholics, that Scripture cannot be proved by itself, because the better known and less known would be the same, can with greater force be turned back against the church.

XIX. If there are those who do not acknowledge the divine quality of Scripture, it is not because the object itself is not knowable or understandable, but because they lack a healthy faculty of reception; from these the gospel is hidden because Satan has blinded their eyes (II Cor. 4:4), like those who deny the existence of God, who is supremely knowable, because they are lacking in understanding, or who do not see the sun because they are blind, as in Seneca's writing a woman who had lost her eyesight kept complaining that the sun had not risen; nonetheless the sun always sends forth its rays, as those who have eyes know from the phenomenon itself.

XX. It is one thing to recognize and proclaim the canon of Scripture; another to establish this canon and make it authoritative. The church cannot do the latter, which is solely the privilege of God, the author. It can do the former, because it is servant, not lord. As a goldsmith who separates dross from the gold, or who seeks gold in the ore, does indeed see the difference between the true and the false, but does not make the true either for himself or for us, so the church by her investigation separates the true canonical books from the noncanonical and apocryphal, but does not make them [canonical], nor could the decision of the church give authority to books which do not have it in themselves, but it proclaims the authority already present by means of arguments from the books themselves.

XXI. Obscure knowledge of a matter is one thing, but distinct knowledge is another. By obscure knowledge the church can be known before Scripture but distinct knowledge of Scripture ought to come first, because the truth about the church can be grasped only from Scripture. Before [we know] Scripture the church may be known to us by "human faith," as an assembly of people using the same forms of worship, but it can be known and trusted as the assembly of the faithful and the communion of the saints, by "divine faith," only after the marks of the church which Scripture supplies have become known.

XXII. When the apostle says that faith comes by hearing (Rom. 10:17) he means only that the ministry of the church ought to be present as the ordinary means of awakening faith in adults, but he does not therefore teach that the church is more knowable than Scripture.

XXIII. It is one thing to raise questions about the number, authors, parts, and particular words of the books of Scripture, and another to raise questions about the fundamental teachings contained in these books. The second form of knowledge, but not the first, is given to every believer, and he who has questions as to who wrote the Gospel of Matthew does not thereby imperil his salvation, if only he believes it to be authentic and of divine quality. Knowing who is the primary author of a book is one thing; knowing who was his secretary is quite another. The latter is a question of historic faith; the former, of true religious faith (*fides divina*).

xxiv. Although, in the language of the philosophers, the "circle" is a sophistic argument, by which something is proved by itself, [an argument] which is developed in a closed series using the same kind of cause recurring within itself, we cannot be accused of such circular reasoning when we prove the Scripture by the Spirit and then prove the Spirit by the Scripture. For there are two different questions, and two different middle terms or kinds of causes: we prove the Scripture by the Spirit, as efficient cause by which we believe, but we prove the Spirit from the Scripture as from the object and argument on account of which we believe. In the first case the question answered is "why, or in virtue of what, do you believe that the Scripture is of divine quality?" In the second, the question is "how, or on account of what, do you believe that the Spirit within you is the Holy Spirit?" The answer is, on account of the marks of the Holy Spirit that are in Scripture. But the Roman Catholics, who accuse us of circular reasoning, obviously fall into it in this matter, when they prove Scripture by the church and the church by Scripture; this is indeed done by the same middle term and the same kind of cause. If we ask them why, or on account of what, they believe the Scripture to have divine quality, they answer, that the church says so. If we ask further why they believe the church, they answer that the Scripture attributes infallibility to it, when it calls it the pillar and bulwark of truth. If we continue, asking why they believe the witness of Scripture to be trustworthy, they reply that the church has made them sure of it. Thus the argument is brought back to where it started, and can go around and around forever, and cannot be fixed in any first believable point. And these are not different kinds of questions; each deals with the ground and argument on account of which I believe, not with the faculty or principle through which I believe.

xxv. The church is called "pillar and bulwark of truth" (I Tim. 3:15), not because it keeps truth from falling and provides authority for it, since truth is rather the foundation of the church, upon which it is built (Eph. 2:20), but [1] because [the Scripture] offers itself and shows itself to the sight of all in the church as on a bulletin board. So "pillar" is used not in its architectural meaning, as pillars are placed to hold up a building, but in its forensic and political meaning, as the edicts of the princes and the decrees and laws of the magistrate used to be posted on pillars in front of the curias and praetoriums, and the doors of [secular] basilicas, so that they might become known by everybody, as Pliny and Josephus report (*Historia Naturalis* 6.28 [(32) 152]; *Antiquities* 1.4 [book 1. 69 − 71]). So the church is the pillar of truth both in the matter of its proclamation, for it is obliged to proclaim the laws of God, and the heavenly truth is posted on her so that it may be known by all, [and pillar] also in the sense of guardian, who not only proclaims the Scripture but also vindicates and protects it, and so it is called not only "pillar," but also "bulwark" (I Tim. 3:15), a support (*firmamentum*) by which known truth is vindicated and preserved, whole and safe against all corruptions, but not a foundation (θεμέλιον; *fundamentum*), which gives truth itself its hypostasis and the basis on which it stands. (2) That which is called pillar and bulwark of truth is not for that reason infallible. The patristic writers (*veteres*) gave this designation to those who surpassed others by excellence of doctrine, or by holiness of life, or firmness of faithful living, and who confirmed the doctrine of the gospel and the Christian faith either by teaching or by example. Thus the believers in Lyons give the designation to Attalus the martyr, according to Eusebius (*Church History* 5.1). Basil gives it to the orthodox bishops who struggled against the Arian heresy—"the pillars and the bulwark of truth" (epistle 120).[13] And Gregory of Nazianzus designates Athanasius in this manner. In the same sense honest and uncorrupted judges in the civil state are called pillars and bulwarks of the laws. (3) This text [I Tim. 3:15] teaches the duty of the church, but not its infallible privilege; what it is supposed to do in the proclamation and defense of truth against all corruptions of its adversaries, not, however, what it always will do, as names are often based on a duty rather than on what is actually done. Malachi 2:7 says that the lips of the priests guard knowledge, which it is their duty to do, although it is not always done, as verse 8 teaches. (4) Whatever is here attributed to the church is attributed to the local church of Ephesus (I Tim. 1:3) to which the Roman Catholics do not attribute the privilege of infallibility, and it refers to the collective church of believers, in which Timothy ought to be included, not the representative one of pastors, much less to the pope, to whom alone they attribute complete freedom from error. (5) Here Paul refers to the use of pillars in the sanctuaries of the pagans, to which either images of the gods, or laws and moral teachings, or oracles, were attached, as Pausanias and Athenaeus tell us, to oppose these pillars of lies and falsehoods, where nothing was present except fables and images of false gods, to the mystic pillar of truth, on which the true image of the invisible God is shown (Col. 1:15), and the heavenly oracles of God are set forth. He also refers to that memorable pillar which Solomon was responsible for setting up in the temple, which is mentioned in II Chronicles 6:13 and II Kings 23:3, upon which, as a platform, the kings mounted whenever they wished to speak to the people,

13. Turretin quotes Basil in Greek, the words being those applied to "the household of God" in the Greek of I Timothy 3:15.

or discharge some important responsibility. It was therefore called "the royal pillar" by the Jews. So truth sits in the church like a queen,[14] not as if she derived her authority from it, just as Solomon did not receive his from this pillar, but because truth is set forth and preserved in the church.

XXVI. The text in Augustine, "I would not be believing the gospel unless the authority of the church convinced me" (*Against the Epistle of Mani Which Is Called Fundamental* 5), does not support the Roman Catholics. (1) Because Augustine speaks of himself while still a Manichean, not yet a Christian, and [here] uses the imperfect where the pluperfect would be expected, "I would not be believing" and "the church convinced" rather than "I would not have believed" and "the church had convinced," a common usage, scholars have noted, among African writers; for example, "if I was desiring those fruits" for "I had desired" (Augustine, *Confessions* 2.8). (2) The authority of which he speaks is not that of law and political power, as our adversaries hold, as if he had believed because the church was telling him to, but an authority of worthiness, founded on the wonderful and most glorious arguments from divine providence which can be seen in the church, such as miracles, antiquity, consensus of different peoples, and continuity, which can lead to faith, but not awaken it as first cause. (3) It is to be noted here, therefore, that it is an external thrust toward faith, and not an infallible source of belief, that Augustine advocates in looking for truth alone, when he tells us that truth is to be preferred above all things, if it is completely proven and cannot be brought into doubt (chap. 4), and when he says, "Let us follow those who invite us first to believe what we cannot yet understand, that,

14. Is enthroned. The image, traditional long before Turretin, is based on Revelation 18:7, "I sit, a queen."

made stronger by this very faith, we may reach the point of knowing what we believe, our minds internally directed and illuminated not by men but by God himself" (chap. 14).[15] So Pierre d'Ailly understands it, and Cano, Gerson, Driedo, and Durand may be understood as upholding the primitive and apostolic church, not the contemporary one, whose authority is here argued. See our disputation on the authority of Scripture.[16]

15. The references continue to be to the tract *Against the Epistle of Mani*. See the *Nicene and Post-Nicene Fathers*, vol. 4, p. 136. Turretin's Latin text is verbally different from the existing printed ones, perhaps quoted from memory.

16. Two *disputationes* under this title, and one, *De circulo pontifico*, about the question of circular reasoning on the proof of Scripture by the church or by the Spirit, are included in volume 4 of Turretin's *Opera*.

The Preservation
of the Canon

QUESTION **7** Will any canonical book ever have disappeared? (Negative)

I. In order more readily to discuss the various questions that are raised concerning the canon, a distinction must first be established. This word is used both broadly and narrowly. In the first sense it was applied by the patristic writers to the ecclesiastical decrees and constitutions, by which the councils and the rulers of the churches were accustomed to specify whatever seemed pertinent to faith, conduct, or discipline. In this are included the various "canons" both of the universal church and of the African, and the collections of canons by Burchard, Ivo, and Gratian, and the canon law itself, which was contained in the codex of canons, in distinction to the divine law which was contained in the codex of Holy Scripture. In the latter sense, "canon" is attributed *par excellence* to Scripture, because God gave it to us as a rule of faith and conduct, in which sense Irenaeus calls it the "unchangeable norm of truth" and Chrysostom the "excellent measure, norm, and rule of all things."

II. Just as the word of God can be seen under two aspects, either as divinely revealed doctrine, or as the sacred books in which it is contained, so also "canon" can be understood in two senses, either of the dogmas, meaning all fundamental teachings, or of the books, meaning all the inspired books. "Canonical Scripture" can be understood in either sense: either as the content of dogmas, because it is the canon and norm of faith and conduct, originally described by the Hebrew word *quoneh*, which means measuring rod, and is so employed in Galatians 6:16 and Philippians 3:16;[1] or with regard to the books, because it contains all the canonical books, in which sense Athanasius at the beginning of his synopsis says that the books of the Christians are not infinite in number, but finite, and comprise a limited canon.

III. The first question regarding the canon is its wholeness, whether any canonical book may have disappeared, or, whether the collection of Scripture as it now is lacks any book which God placed in the canon. On this matter both the Roman Catholics and the Reformed (*orthodoxi*) divide into different groups. Many Roman Catholics maintain that a number of canonical books have disappeared, so that they may show the imperfection of Scripture and the necessity of the tradition by which the gaps may be filled. Some of our theologians, such as Musculus and Whittaker, teach the same thing, following Chrysostom, but with two reservations; first, they affirm this only with regard to some books of the Old Testament, not any of the New, as do Roman Catholics; second, they maintain that nothing is taken away from the perfection of Scripture, which the Roman Catholics attack, by this, because the wholeness of the canon is not measured by the number of the sacred books, or their quantitative perfection, but by

1. Its presumed Greek equivalent κανών (Vulgate, *regula*) is employed in these texts to refer to the faith. The clause containing κανών in Philippians 3:16 is omitted from modern critical editions, but is part of the Vulgate and the King James Version.

the completeness of the dogmas and the essential perfection of all things necessary for salvation, which is amply found in the existing books. But the more common and wiser opinion is that of others, who hold that no genuinely canonical books have disappeared, and that if any books have, they were not endowed with this quality.

IV. The reasons are to be sought (1) from the witness of Christ, who said that it was easier for heaven and earth to pass away than for one jot of the law to perish (Matt. 5:18; Luke 16:17). But if not even a jot, or the smallest mark, can perish, how could several books vanish? Although Christ is speaking of the teaching of the law, not the books, yet this can be applied to the sacred books by analogy, and their immunity from destruction can be affirmed, the more so because not only is reference made to the letters and marks by which Scripture is written, but also God willed that this teaching be preserved in written books. (2) From the statements of Luke and Paul. For neither could Luke have spoken of all the prophets and all the Scripture (Luke 24:27) if any part of them had disappeared, nor could Paul have said, "Whatever ... was written was for our instruction" (Rom. 15:4), unless he assumed that the whole written Old Testament was in existence.

V. (3) From the providence of God, who always keeps watch for the continuing safety of the church. It cannot be conceived that providence would will that such a destructive loss occur; what would become of the wisdom, goodness, and power of God if he willed that such a precious treasure be shown to his church and then withdrawn, and that the body of Scripture exist now in a torn and wounded state?[2] (4) From the duty of the church, which is commissioned to preserve zealously the oracles of God for herself.

2. As often, the argument depends not on previous demonstration (the attributes of God are discussed in the next locus) but on doctrines basic to the system as a whole.

That this commission was not neglected is evident from the fact that neither Christ nor the apostles ever accuse the Jews of this, a sacrilege which those who do not overlook lesser ones would by no means have hidden, if [the Jews] had been guilty of it; indeed, Paul emphasizes this privilege of the Jews—that the oracles of God were entrusted to them (Rom. 3:2; 9:4).[3] (5) From the destiny (*fines*) of Scripture which is sealed in the canon of faith and life even to the consummation of the age. This could not be so if only a mutilated and truncated canon were left for the church of this age, because of the loss of some canonical books; that is, it would be impossible without the canon. (6) From the custom of the Jews, because books of the canon of the Old Testament other than those which appear in our canon were never recognized, or interpreted in the Targum, or translated in the Septuagint.

VI. Not everything which men of God ever wrote was of divine quality and inspired. They were able, as human beings, to reflect upon some events and interpret them with care, and [to record] others, as prophets, by divine inspiration as authoritative for faith; matters which fall into the first category can be freely investigated, but those of the second must be believed, as Augustine well says (*City of God* 18.38).[4] Just as not everything they said was canonical, so was not everything they wrote. If Solomon wrote a number of books of parables and songs, and about plants and animals (I Kings 4:22 − 23), it does not follow that they were canonical. They could have been prepared as a result of human study, to make public the manifold knowledge of nature which he possessed, without being of divine wisdom and supernatural inspiration.

3. Like some other Protestant writers, Turretin seems ready to suggest that more faithfulness can be found among Jews, over their entire pre-Christian history, than in the Christian church as known in much of its history.

4. *Nicene and Post-Nicene Fathers*, vol. 2, p. 383.

VII. The books which are said to have disappeared either were not sacred and canonical, like the *Book of the Wars of Jehovah* (Num. 21:14; Josh. 10:15 [13])[5] or the *Book of the Upright* (II Sam. 1:14 [18]), and the *Chronicles of the Kings of Judah and Israel* (I Kings. 14:19 – 20; 15:7), which are not concerned with the teachings of religion, but are either secular annals, in which the actions of the Israelites are recorded, or lists of official acts and civil laws, as is plain from I Kings 11:41. Or, the books which are said to have disappeared are extant under other names, like the books of Gad and Nathan (II Chron. 29:29 [25]), of Iddo (II Chron. 9:29),[6] and of Shemaiah and Iddo (II Chron. 12:15). The Jews teach, and some of the patristic writers observe, that these make up parts of the Books of Samuel and Kings, and some Roman Catholics of good standing agree—Sixtus Senensis, Paul Burgensis, Lewis de Tena, Sanctius, and others.

VIII. The book of the Lord mentioned in Isaiah 34:16 is nothing other than the prophecy which he was writing in the name of the Lord, and which therefore he called the book of the Lord. Jeremiah's book mourning the death of King Josiah (II Chron. 35:25) can still be read in Lamentations.

IX. It is not said in Colossians 4:16 that there was any letter of Paul to the Laodiceans, for it speaks of a letter from, not to, the Laodiceans, which could have been by the Laodiceans to Paul, who wanted it to be read by the Colossians along with his because he knew that there were in it matters of concern to them. Whence it is evident how unreasonable was Faber Stapulensis's desire to give the

5. Clearly a lapse of memory. Joshua 10:13 refers to the Book of Jashar (or the Upright). (Both the Utrecht and the Edinburgh editions read as translated.)
6. Turretin writes (*liber*) *Jehdonis* for II Chronicles 9:29 and *Hiddonis* for 12:15. The Vulgate reads *Addo* in both places. The variant readings in the Septuagint and the Hebrew seem irrelevant to this.

epistle to the Laodiceans to the Christian world, as the more prudent Roman Catholics admit.

x. In Jude 14 there is no mention of a book of Enoch, but only of his prophecy, for he is said to have prophesied, not written; if he did write a book it is evident that it was never included in the canon, both from the silence of Josephus and Jerome, and from the fact that Moses is recorded as the first canonical writer (Luke 24:27). It does appear from Augustine (*City of God* 15.13 [24])[7] that in his day there was an apocryphal book of which Enoch was considered the author, a fragment of which Scaliger has given us in his commentary on Eusebius.

xi. If some of the apostles mention passages of the Old Testament which cannot now be found explicitly in any canonical book, it does not follow that some canonical book, in which these words were written, has disappeared. At times the words are present implicitly and by intention. What is said of Christ in Matthew 2:23—that he will be called a Nazarene—is based either, as Jerome supposed, on Isaiah 11:7 [1], where Christ is called a branch,[8] or on Judges 13:5, which says that Samson, a type of Christ, will be a Nazarene of God from his mother's womb.[9] In what is said in I Corinthians 5:9 about a letter that [Paul] had written them, there is no reason why we should not understand the letter which he was writing, in which, somewhat earlier, he had told them that those who polluted themselves by incest should be excommunicated, as in Colossians 4:16, "when the letter has been read," namely, the letter that he was writing. Or [references] are merely historical, like that of Jude 9, concerning the devil's struggle

7. *Nicene and Post-Nicene Fathers*, vol. 2, p. 305.

8. Jerome's theory was based on phonetic resemblances between the Hebrew for "branch" and "Nazarene."

9. "Nazarite" (Judg. 13:5, RSV) is *nazaraeus* in the Latin; the same word is used in Latin in Matthew 2:23 (RSV, "Nazarene").

with Michael over the body of Moses, which could rest either on tradition, as some scholars hold, or on some noncanonical ecclesiastical book which has disappeared. XII. Although the autographs of the Law and the Prophets which were kept in the ark could have been burned along with it when the city was destroyed and the temple burned at the time of the Babylonian captivity, it does not follow from this that all the sacred books, to be rewritten afresh by Ezra, as by a second Moses, in forty days, were destroyed at that time. A number of copies could have remained among the pious, on the basis of which the worship of God was later set up (Ezra 6:18; Neh. 8:2). Nor is it likely that Ezekiel and the pious priests, and also Jeremiah, Gedeliah, and Baruch, who received permission to remain in Judea, would have been without them, especially since the care and reading of the sacred books was their duty; in the case of Daniel this is plainly seen (Dan. 9:2). IV Esdras 4:23 and 14:21, on the basis of which a universal destruction has been claimed, prove nothing because they are apocryphal even to the Roman Catholics, and are refuted by another apocryphal book that is canonical to them— I Maccabees 2:4 [II Maccabees 2:4 − 5], which says that the ark in which the book of the law was kept (Deut. 31:26) was preserved by Jeremiah in a cave on Mount Nebo. Above all, the great silence of Scripture, which since it bewails with such agony the pollution of the sanctuary, the fall of Jerusalem, the removal of the sacred vessels, the destruction of the temple, and other events, could not have omitted such a great loss without open lamentation, refutes this falsehood [of the destruction of Scripture]. Ezra therefore could engage in collating, correcting, and restoring the copies which had been damaged during the captivity, which he could most appropriately do as an inspired person, but it was not his task to give [Scripture] anew to the church.

The Canonicity
of the Old Testament

QUESTION **8**

Are the books of the Old Testament still part of the canon of faith, and the rule of conduct in the church of the New Testament? (Affirmative, against the Anabaptists)

I. This question divides us from the Anabaptists, who exclude the Old Testament books from the canon of faith, as if they were of little consequence for Christians, or as if dogmas of faith and precepts for life ought not to be drawn from them. The Mennonites teach in their confession that all Christians, according as they have acquired faith, must of necessity conform solely to the gospel of Christ (article 11), and this was confirmed at the colloquy of Frankenthal. The Reformed (*orthodoxi*), on the other hand, hold that the Old Testament is no less the concern of Christians than the New, and that dogmas of faith and the regulation of life are to be based on both (French Confession, articles 4 and 5; Swiss Confession, article 1).[1]

1. Turretin's words would apply to the first article of either the First or Second Swiss (Helvetic) Confession. The Mennonite confession here cited is one whose text I have not seen. That there is prejudice against Mennonites in Turretin, as in other "main line" writers of his time, cannot be disputed. In this question, however, in a very formal, scholastic way he deals with a vital question about the use of Scripture. The difference between Reformed and Anabaptist thought on such basic issues as civil authority, war, the oath, and,

II. It is not a question of the Old Testament in the sense of the Mosaic economy; indeed we believe that this has been so abrogated by Christ that it no longer deserves a place in the economy of grace. But there is a question about it as to teaching, whether there is still use for it under the New Testament as canon of faith and conduct.

III. It is not here a question whether Christ has reformed the law given in the Old Testament by correcting and completing it (this will be discussed later against the Socinians),[2] but whether the Old Testament so applies to Christians that the canon of faith and rule of life should be sought and proved from it no less than from the New Testament, and that the religion of Christ is contained in Moses and the prophets no less than in the books of the New Testament, and can be demonstrated from them, which the adversaries deny, and we affirm.

IV. The difference between the Old and New Testaments is not in question, nor that of the teachings which proceed from both; we do not deny that the teaching of the New Testament is much clearer than that of the Old, both because of the types in which that of the Old is given, and because of the predictions and promises which are given in it. The question concerns the principle of the Christian

because of the analogy of circumcision, infant baptism, came to a head in such different practical uses of the Old Testament that, from Turretin's point of view, the Anabaptists had in fact "decanonized" it. The Reformed view of the unity of Scripture, a point at issue also with Lutherans because of differences regarding the law, is well illustrated here.

2. Turretin does not return to this topic in this locus. He takes it up in various later parts of the work, for example, locus 11 (*De lege Dei*), question 3, where Christ's relationship to the law is discussed "against the Socinians, Remonstrants, Anabaptists, and Papists," and locus 12 (*De foedere gratia*), where the unity of the covenant of grace in both Testaments is argued "against the Socinians, Anabaptists, and Remonstrants." What Christ did to the law is crucial in both cases.

faith (*religio*)—whether this is found only in the New Testament books, or also, which we affirm, in the Old.[3]

v. The reasons are (1) Christ approved the Old Testament and wanted Moses and the prophets to be heard by believers (Luke 16:29). This was not said to Jews to the exclusion of others, for here a general precept is given to all who want to avoid eternal punishment, and what is here given as a precept is recommended to Christians as practice by Peter: "We have the prophetic word made more sure, to which you do well to attend, as to a light shining in a dark place, until the day breaks and the morning star rises in your hearts" (II Peter 1:19). Nor can exception be taken on the ground that a qualification is added by Peter, that this attending to the prophets holds only until the time of the New Testament, when the day had broken, for [even] if he refers to the New Testament, the value of the prophetic word is not restricted, according to this text, to the time previous to the New Testament, because "until" is not always used of an action that is completed so as to exclude any future action, as is shown by a number of passages (Gen. 28:15; Matt. 28:30 [20]; I Cor. 15:25). If it refers to the day of eternal life, and the rising of the morning star in the region of glory, which is in truth the day *par excellence*, and which seems more probable because he writes to believers who had already received faith in equal measure, and so in whose hearts the day of grace and the morning star of the gospel had already arisen, then our

3. Turretin's understanding of the place of the Old Testament is grounded in his concept of the unity of revelation. He has little sense of historical development, and regards the Old Testament as a book about Christ as well as about God's requirements for human life. Hence, the importance of typology in his exegesis, and his constant emphasis on the obscurity of the Old Testament. It is obscure and typological about Christ, although containing the same truths about him as the New.

argument gains strength; that is to say, the prophetic words must be heeded to the end of the age, until that blessed day dawns which is true day, everlasting and not ended by night.

VI. (2) The church of the New Testament is built on the foundation of the prophets and the apostles (Eph. 2:20); that is, of the teaching of prophets and apostles. The New Testament prophets mentioned in Ephesians 3:5 and I Corinthians 12:28 cannot be understood here, because the passage deals with the permanent foundation of the universal church, while the New Testament prophetic gift was temporary; nor does the order of the words (*ordo collectionis*) imply priority in time or duration, as in Ephesians 4:12 the New Testament prophets are listed before the evangelists, although they did not come before them in time.[4]

VII. (3) "Whatever was written in former days was written for our instruction, that by steadfastness and by the encouragement of the scriptures we might have hope" (Rom. 15:4). Although all things in Scripture are not of the same nature and use, yet all are of the same origin and authority, equally given for the welfare and edification of the church.

VIII. (4) The canon of the Old Testament is sufficient for faith and conduct, and those sacred writings in which Timothy was instructed from his youth, when the canon of the New Testament had not yet been written, could make him wise unto salvation (II Tim. 3:14 – 15). And if the man of God, that is, the minister of the gospel, can be equipped for every good work by them, they are much more useful and necessary for the faith of the private person, and for the direction of his life. Nor does Paul here

4. Turretin's reason for emphasizing this argument about chronology would have been more evident had he used the word order of Ephesians 2:20— "apostles and prophets"—in the first sentence.

refer only to the time before the writing of the New Testament, because he speaks in general of all inspired Scripture (v. 16).

IX. (5) Christ dismisses the Jews that they may study the Scriptures (John 5:39), since they are the source of life. This is not spoken to the Jews merely as a description of what they were doing, but as a commandment, because (1) Christ's purpose was to lead the Jews to the reading of Scripture as a means of bringing them to a knowledge of himself, and a witness [to him] greater than any objection, and (2) granting that Christ spoke in the indicative, the substance [of our argument] is the same, because he approved their practice [of reading the Old Testament] and did not rebuke it.

X. (6) The Old Testament Scripture contains the same substance of doctrine as the New, both with regard to things to be believed, and to be done, nor is any other gospel proclaimed today to us than which was formerly promised in the prophetic writings (Rom. 1:3 [2]; 16:25 — 26). So Paul, who proclaimed the whole plan of God for salvation to Christians (Acts 20:26 [27]) declared that he had taught nothing except what was spoken by Moses and the prophets (Acts 26:22). Nor is any other law prescribed for us besides that which was formerly brought by Moses, which required love of God and neighbor (Matt. 22:37 — 39).

XI. (7) If the Old Testament does not apply to Christians, it cannot be convincingly proved to Jews that Jesus Christ of Nazareth is the true Messiah, because only by comparing the Scriptures, and by the correspondence of the predictions of the Messiah in the Old Testament to their fulfillment in our Jesus under the New, which was more than once shown by Christ and the apostles (Luke 24:27, 44; Acts 10:43; 17:11; 26:22; Rom. 3:21), can this be done.

XII. By the law and the prophets which were to remain until John (Matt. 11:12 [13]), the books of the Old Testament and their permanence are not to be understood, compared to that of the New. The first was prophetic, the second evangelical; the first is of shadows and types which promise a Messiah who is to be given, the second is clear and plain, which proclaims a Messiah who has been given. Christ says that these two modes of revelation are to be brought together: the first, [revelation] through prophecy, to last only until John, because after the Messiah had been given he no longer wanted to be proclaimed as to come; the other, [revelation] through the evangelizing that declares that Christ has come, began with John.

XIII. When the apostles are called ministers of the Spirit, not of the letter (II Cor. 3:5 — 6), by "letter" the books of the Old Testament are not to be understood, as if they should no longer be used, since on the contrary they used them constantly, but the legal economy, as contrasted to the evangelical [should be understood]. It is in many ways superior, not only because of its clarity and completeness, but also because of its efficacy, because it not only requires and commands duty as does the law, but also performs it through the law written in hearts by the Spirit.

XIV. It is one thing for the old covenant to be out of date with regard to mode of administration and the incidental aspects (*accidentia*) of the covenant, or the external accompaniments of matters therewith, which is what Paul affirms (Heb. 8:13), but it is another for it to be so with regard to what is administered and its substance, or the internal form of the covenant itself, which is what we deny.

XV. It is one thing to speak of the obligation of the ceremonies of the Old Testament, or the law concerning them, and another of the permanence of both the knowledge of and meditation upon the books of the Law and the Prophets. Because the law has only the shadow of blessings to come it does not apply to Christians, who have the express image of these [blessings], as a matter of practice and observance; it can, however, apply as a matter of teaching and knowledge, and as illustration of that image (*quoad relationem ad* τὴν εἰκόνα). Indeed the content (*corpus*) shows forth more clearly from the correspondence between the revealed shadows and forms.

XVI. Christ, in Matthew 5, does not dispute against Moses and the precepts of the law itself, but rather acts as interpreter and vindicator of the law, by rejecting corruptions and glosses which Jewish teachers had attached to it, and restoring its splendor and true meaning, as will be seen specifically in the locus about the law.[5]

XVII. Although the New Testament Scripture is complete in an intensive sense, with regard to the substance of saving doctrine, it is not complete in the extensive sense, with regard to the full breadth of divine revelation, because it speaks only of Christ as having been revealed, not of him as to be revealed, a form of witness that is most useful for the confirmation of faith. So the perfection of the books of the New Testament does not exclude the use of the books of the Old, both because the New Testament itself witnesses that it rests upon the Old, and because the repetition of many testimonies to the same fact is a valid witness for us, and increases assurance of our faith.

XVIII. Anything that does not come, either directly or indirectly, from Christ does not have authority for Christians. But the law that was given by Moses was also given by Christ; by Moses as servant (*servus*), by Christ as Lord. So in Acts 7:38 the same angel who appeared to Moses in the desert (v. 30), and who was Jehovah himself (Exod. 3:2), is said to have spoken to Moses on Mount Sinai, because the Son of God, who is called the angel of the covenant and of the presence, was the primary author and promulgator of the law, of which Moses was only a servant

5. Locus 11 (not translated).

(*minister*). This does not destroy the distinction between the promulgation of the law and of the gospel, because in the law the Son of God worked only indirectly and as disincarnate, but is called the first author of the gospel directly and as incarnate (Heb. 2:3).

XIX. Christ is called the end of the law (Rom. 10:4), both because he was the purpose (*scopus*) toward which the entire law looked, and because he was its realization and completion, not by doing away with its value, but by fulfilling its oracles, and carrying them out, both in his own person, by action and by suffering, and in his people, by inscribing the law on the hearts of believers, whence he is said to have come not to destroy the law, but to fulfill it (Matt. 5:17).

XX. Servants are not to be listened to, if they say anything contrary to, or injurious to, the master when he is absent, but they can and should be heard if they speak about him in accordance with his commandment. Moses and the prophets did this no less than the apostles (John 5:46; Acts 10:43), and Christ expressly enjoins the hearing of Moses and the prophets (Luke 16:29). This is not going back from Christ to Moses, but a going forward from Moses, who is tutor (Gal. 3:24), to Christ.

XXI. The beginning of John's preaching is properly called the beginning of the gospel (Mark 1:1) with regard to fulfillment and with respect to the revelation of Christ as sent, but not with regard to the promise and with respect to [the revelation of] Christ as one to be sent, which had been given previously under the Old Testament (Rom. 1:2; Gal. 3:8; Isa. 52:7; 61:1).

The Canonicity
of the Apocrypha

QUESTION **9**

Are Tobit, Judith, Wisdom, Ecclesiasticus, the first two books of Maccabees, Baruch, and the additions to Esther and Daniel properly included in the list of canonical books? (Negative, against the Roman Catholics)

I. The apocryphal books are so called not because the authors of the books are unknown—there are canonical works whose authors are not known and apocryphal ones whose authors are—nor because they are read only privately, and not in public [worship]; some of them are indeed read in public. They are so called either because they were kept out of the chest in which the sacred writings were preserved, as Epiphanius and Augustine supposed, or because their authority was unclear and suspect and therefore their use was restricted, that is, the church did not read them for the purpose of establishing ecclesiastical dogmas, as Jerome says in his preface to the Proverbs of Solomon; or, which is the more truthful explanation, because they are of doubtful and obscure origin, and the obscurity was not cleared up by those through whose testimony the authority of Scripture came to us, as Augustine says (*City of God* 5.24 [15.23]).

II. The question does not involve the books of the Old and New Testaments which we regard as canonical; these the Roman Catholics also accept. Nor does it involve all apocryphal writings; there are some which the Roman Catholics reject no less than we, such as III and IV Esdras, III and IV Maccabees, or the prayer of Manassas.[1] But we are concerned with Tobit, Judith, Baruch, Wisdom, Ecclesiasticus, I and II Maccabees, and the additions to Esther and Daniel, which the Roman Catholics include among the canonical writings. We exclude them, not that they are without many true and pious elements, but that they lack the marks of the canonical books.

III. There are a number of reasons. (1) The Jewish church, to which was entrusted the oracles of God (Rom. 3:2), did not accept them, using the same canon as we, as Josephus witnesses (*Against Apion* 1. [8]) and as Becanus and Stapleton admit. This could not have been done without serious sin (*crimen*) if these books had been entrusted to them on the same terms as the others, but no such charge is ever made against them by Christ or by the apostles. At this point no distinction ought to be made between the Jewish and the Christian canon, because Christians cannot and should not accept any books as canonical, except those accepted by the Jews, their book-carriers (*capsarii*), as Augustine calls them—"who carry the books for us students" (commentary on Psalm 60). (2) [The apocryphal books] are never cited as canonical by Christ and the apostles as the others are, and indeed when Christ divides all the Old Testament books into three classes—law, psalms, and prophets (Luke 24:44)—he obviously gave his approval to the Jewish canon, and excluded those books which are not contained in this classification. (3) Because the Christian church accepted the same canon as we, and no other books, for four hundred years; this is shown by the canons of the Council of Laodicea (59), by Melito, bishop of Sardis,

1. They appear in the Clementine Vulgate as an appendix.

who lived in A.D. 116 (Eusebius, *Church History* 4.25),[2] Epiphanius in his treatment of the Epicureans, Jerome in his prologue, Athanasius in his synopsis. (4) Because the authors [of the Apocrypha] were not prophets and inspired men, since these books were written after Malachi, the last of the prophets, nor were they written in Hebrew, like the Old Testament, but in Greek. So Josephus says, in the place cited above, that the writings of his people after the time of Artaxerxes are not of equal trustworthiness and authority with the earlier ones, as not being in the true succession of the prophets.

IV. (5) Both the style and the content of these books cry out that they are human, not divine, so that anyone who did not realize that they were produced by human effort would be a person of little insight, although some [of the books] are superior to others. For besides the fact that the style does not equal the majesty and simplicity of the divine style, but is redolent of the evil and weakness of human learning, with folly, flattery, conceit, affectation, pseudoerudition and false eloquence, all of which occur frequently (*non raro*), there is in [these books] so much that is not only inconsequential and frivolous, but also false, superstitious, and contradictory, that it is very plain that [these books] were of human, not divine, composition. We give a few examples of the many errors. In Tobit lying is attributed to the angel, who in 5:15 [12] calls himself Azariah the son of Ananias, and in 12:15 Raphael the angel of the Lord. The same [angel] in chapter 6 gives magical guidance for the expulsion of a demon by the smoke of a burning fish's liver, contrary to the word of Christ (Matt. 17:21). He accepts for himself the offering of prayer which is rightful only for Christ (12:12). The book of Judith praises

2. This date is given in Turretin's text. Modern scholarship gives an approximate date of A.D. 160.

(9:2) an act of Simeon that was cursed by Jacob (Gen. 49 [:5 – 7]); it praises the lying and deception of Judith, which is not consistent with piety (chap. 11); and worse than that, it praises her for seeking the blessing of God for her lying and deception (9:13). There is no mention of the city of Bethulia in Scripture, nor is there any mention of this deliverance [by Judith] in either Josephus or Philo, who wrote about Jewish history. The author of Wisdom falsely states that he was king in Israel (9:7 – 8), and is understood as Solomon, although he mentions athletic contests which were not yet being held among the Greeks of Solomon's time (4:2); moreover, he presents the Pythagorean doctrine of transmigration (8:19 – 20) and gives a false account of the origin of idols (15:15 – 16). The son of Sirach attributes to Samuel an act that was the work of an evil demon called forth by wicked methods (Ecclesiasticus 46:20; I Sam. 28:11), gives a false account of the corporeal return of Elijah (*de Elia corporaliter reverso*) (48:11), and, in the prologue, apologizes for his delusions.

v. In the additions to Esther and Daniel there are so many contradictory and foolish statements that Sixtus Senensis simply rejects them. Baruch says that he read his book to Jeconiah and all the people in Babylon in the fifth year after the fall of Jerusalem (Baruch 1:2 – 3), when, however, Jeconiah was still in prison, and Baruch was in Egypt, taken away with [Jeremiah][3] after the assassination of Gedaliah (Jer. 43:10 [7]). The altar of the Lord is mentioned at a time when the temple no longer existed (Baruch 1:10). The books of the Maccabees often contradict each other—compare I Maccabees 1:16 with 9:5 and 28, and I Maccabees 10. The suicide of Razis is praised (II Maccabees 14:42). Will-worship is praised when Judas [Maccabeus] offers

3. *Cum Jechoniah*, the reading of the Utrecht and Edinburgh editions, cannot have been intended.

sacrifices for the dead which are not provided for by the law (II Maccabees 12:42). The author apologizes for his weakness and infirmity, and comments on the difficulty of stitching together his patchwork (*cento*) out of the five books of Jason of Cyrene (II Maccabees 2:24; 15:[38 —]39).[4] If anyone should want more on these books, let him consult Rainold, Chamierus, Molinaeus, Spanheim, and others who have carried on this discussion extensively and soundly.

VI. The canon of faith is one thing; the canon of ecclesiastical reading is another. We are not discussing the latter, for it is well known that these apocryphal books have from time to time been read in public worship, but only for the instruction of the people, as Jerome says in his preface to the book of Solomon. Likewise the "legends," which are so called from *legendum*,[5] and which told of the sufferings of the martyrs, used to be read in public worship, although not regarded as canonical. Here we are discussing the canon of faith.

VII. The word *canon* is used in two senses by the patristic writers, broadly and narrowly. In the former sense it includes not only the canon of faith but also that of ecclesiastical reading. In this sense the forty-seventh canon of the third Council of Carthage must be understood, when it calls the books [of the Apocrypha] canonical, not narrowly and with strict accuracy as the canon of faith, but broadly as the canon of reading, as the synod, which also desired that the "passions of the martyrs" be read, explicitly

4. Turretin cannot imagine the Apocrypha being revelation, because of its contradiction of much of his polemics and also his ethics. Not only revulsion at the adoration of creatures, but also special emphasis on "absolute" truthtelling (as against "Jesuit equivocation," cf. Westminster Confession 22.4), and opposition to voluntary self-destruction even in the performance of military duty all are topics of emphasis in his exposition of the Decalogue (locus 11).

5. "To be read."

declared (if indeed this canon is not interpolated, since it mentions Pope Boniface, who at that time was not yet pope, so that Syrius Monachus calls this a canon of the seventh council of Carthage, not the third). Augustine is to be understood in the same way when he calls [the Apocrypha] canonical. He sets up two classes of canons, one that is accepted by all churches and concerning which there is no question; the second which is accepted by some, and which was commonly read by both parties, and he held this second as not to be esteemed as much as the first, and its authority to be much less (*Against the Manicheans* 2.5). The Apocrypha indeed are for him corrupt, false, and dishonest writings; he calls them "fables of scriptures which are called apocrypha" (*City of God* 5.24 [15.23]). But "canon" is used narrowly for that which had divine and infallible authority for proving the dogmas of the faith, and thus Jerome uses the word when he excludes [the Apocrypha] from the canon. So Augustine uses the word *canon* more broadly than Jerome, who uses the word *apocrypha* more broadly than Augustine, not only for books which are clearly false and mythological, but also for those which, although read in church, are not employed for proving the dogmas of the faith, so that it is easy to harmonize the words of these Fathers, who seem to disagree in this matter. So Cajetan, at the end of his commentary on Esther, explains the words of the Fathers: "for Jerome the words of councils and fathers are reduced to such a classification that they are not canonical, that is, containing rules for the establishment of articles of faith, although they can be called canonical, that is, containing rules for the edification of believers, since they are received into the biblical canon for this purpose," with which teaching Dionysius the Carthusian agrees in his preface to Tobit.

VIII. There is no point to the Roman Catholic distinction between the canon of the Jews and that of the Christians, for, although our canon in its totality means all the books of the Old and New Testaments, which are equally part of it, as is not the case with the Jews, who reject the New, nevertheless, if the word is used of a part, that is, the Old Testament, in which sense we are now discussing, it is certain that our canon does not differ from that of the Jews, because they have never received any books into the canon except those which we do.

IX. If among the Fathers there is reference to some deuterocanonical works, it is not to be understood that they are in truth and univocally canonical with respect to faith, but they are included in the canon of reading, on account of many pious and useful contents that can serve for edification.

X. The quotation of a passage does not prove a book to be canonical, (1) for if it did, Aratus, Menander, and Epimenides, who are quoted by Paul (Acts 17:28; I Cor. 15:33; Titus 1:12) would be canonical, and (2) the words which our adversaries claim are quoted from the Apocrypha can be found in other canonical books, from which, rather than from the Apocrypha, the apostles could have quoted.

XI. If [the apocryphal books] are joined to the canonical ones, it does not follow that they are of equal authority, but only that they are useful for the cultivation of morals, and for an understanding of the history of [biblical] times, not for the establishment of faith.[6]

XII. Although some apocryphal books, such as Wisdom and Ecclesiasticus, are better and purer than others, and

6. Most Protestant Bibles, in Turretin's time and long afterward, followed Luther's practice and included the Apocrypha. Turretin in other places explicitly recommends historical study as an aid to understanding the Bible, and doubtless welcomed the reading of the apocryphal books in Christian families for that purpose. It will also be noted that he would oppose their "false and superstitious" teachings not by censorship, but by reason and the work of the Spirit.

contain a number of ethical teachings of good content, which have their value, yet because they have many other teachings both false and foolish, they are wisely excluded from the canon.

XIII. Although some doubted the authenticity of a number of New Testament books, such as the Epistle of James, II Peter, II and III John, and Revelation, which afterward were held canonical by the church, it does not follow that this could happen with respect to the apocryphal books, because in this matter the status of Old and New Testament books is different. (1) For the books of the Old Testament were not given to the Christian church by stages, in temporal succession or through parts of the church, but all books belonging to it were received from the Jews at one and the same time written in one codex, after they had received unquestioned authority, which was confirmed by Christ himself and by the apostles. But the books of the New Testament were written separately in different times and places, and gradually collected into one corpus. Therefore, some of the later books, which came later to some churches, especially in remote areas, were held in doubt by some, until their authenticity gradually became known. (2) Although some Epistles and the Book of Revelation were questioned in some churches, yet there were always many more that accepted them. But there was never any disagreement over the apocryphal books, because they were always rejected by the Jewish church.

The Purity
of the Original Text

QUESTION **10** Has the original text of the Old and New Testaments come to us pure and uncorrupted? (Affirmative, against the Roman Catholics)

I. This question is forced upon us by the Roman Catholics, who raise doubts concerning the purity of the sources in order more readily to establish the authority of their Vulgate and lead us to the tribunal of the church.

II. By "original texts" we do not mean the very autographs from the hands of Moses, the prophets, and the apostles, which are known to be nonexistent. We mean copies (*apographa*), which have come in their name, because they record for us that word of God in the same words into which the sacred writers committed it under the immediate inspiration of the Holy Spirit.

III. There is no question of the sources being pure in the sense that no error has crept into many sacred codices, either from the ravages of time, or the carelessness of copyists, or the malice of Jews and heretics. This is recognized on both sides, and the variant readings, which Beza and Robert Stephanus have noted in Greek, and the Jews in Hebrew, witness sufficiently to this. But the question is whether the original text, in Hebrew or in Greek, has been so corrupted, either by the carelessness of copyists or by the malice of Jews and heretics, that it can no longer be held as the judge of controversies and the norm by which all versions without exception are to be judged. The Roman Catholics affirm this; we deny it.

IV. Not all Roman Catholics are of this opinion. There are many, who are called Hebraists, who uphold the purity of the sources, and defend it explicitly, among them Sixtus Senensis, Bannes, Andradius, Driedo, Arias Montanus, John Isaac, Jacob Bonfrerius, Simeon de Muis, and many others. Others, however, maintain strongly the corruption of the sources; among them, Stapleton, Lindanus, Cano, Cotton, Morinus, Perronius, Gordon, and others. There are some who, following a middle road, assert neither that the sources are corrupt nor that they flow with purity and integrity, so that they maintain everything must be studied and emended in connection with the versions. This is the teaching of Bellarmine (*De Verbo Dei* 2.2), who on this matter, as on others, must be understood as inconsistent.

V. That the sources are not corrupt is demonstrated by (1) the providence of God, which would not allow (*cui repugnat*) that the books which he had willed to be written by inspired men for the salvation of the human race, and which he willed to remain to the end of the world so that the waters of salvation[1] could be drawn from them, should be so falsified that they would be useless for that purpose. And since new revelations are not to be expected after God has committed his whole will concerning the doctrine of salvation to the books of Scripture, what could be more derogatory to God, who has promised always to be with his church, than to assert that the books in which this doctrine is preserved have been corrupted so that they cannot be the canon of faith? (2) The faithfulness of the Christian church, and its diligent work in preserving Scrip-

1. Isaiah 12:3.

ture. Since Christians always watched over it with great
care, to preserve the sacred deposit unharmed, it is un-
believable that they either falsified it or allowed anyone
else to do so. (3) The religion of the Jews, which looked
upon the sacred codices with great faith and concern, to
the point of superstition, so that Josephus could say that
after the passage of centuries no one dared add to or sub-
tract from or change the books of the Jews, and that among
them it was almost instinctive to be prepared to die for
Scripture (*Against Apion*, book 2). Philo in his work on the
exodus of the children of Israel from Egypt, quoted by
Eusebius, goes further when he states that, up to his time,
during a period of more than two thousand years, no word
in the Hebrew law was changed, and that any number of
Jews would rather die than allow the law to undergo any
change (*Preparation for the Gospel* 8.2). Indeed, they were
overcome with foolish superstition about the sacred codex,
so that if a written book of the law touched the ground
they proclaimed a fast, and they said that it was to be
feared that the universe would revert to primeval chaos—
so far were they from allowing fraud with the sacred codices. (4) The care with which the Masoretes not only counted,
but recorded in writing, all variations in pointing and writing, not only with regard to verses and words, but to individual letters, so that there could be neither place for,
nor suspicion of, forgers, an argument used by Arias Montanus in his biblical preface. (5) The large number of copies.
Since the sacred codices are so widely scattered, how could
all of them have been corrupted either by the carelessness
of copyists or by the malice of falsifiers? "Far be it," as
Augustine says, "from any prudent man to believe that the
Jews, however perverse and evil-minded, could have done
this with so many and widely scattered copies" (*City of
God* 15.2 [13]). Vives says that this argument should be
used against those who "argue that the Hebrew manu-

scripts of the Old Testament and the Greek of the New have been falsified and corrupted, so that the truth of the sacred books cannot be found in them."

VI. (6) If the sources were corrupted, it was done either before or after Christ. Neither is possible. Not before, for Christ never suggested it when he discussed various errors of doctrine, and he would not have upheld the use of corrupted books. Was the Lord so indifferent to the salvation of his people that he never even mentioned, personally or through the apostles, that the books of Moses and the prophets were falsified, when at the same time he refuted the Jews from these same books (but in vain, if they were corrupted and changed), and summoned and urged his disciples to read and examine them? Not afterward, both because the copies scattered among Christians would have made such effort useless, and also because there is no trace of such corruption. For if anything of the kind had taken place, why are the passages which Christ and the apostles quote from Moses and the prophets the same today and always, and not corrupted at all? Why did Origen and Jerome, who had magnificent knowledge of the sacred languages, so specifically absolve the Jews from this wrong? Therefore if the corruption was not done either before or after Christ, it follows that it was never done, an argument that Bellarmine brings forward (*De Verbo Dei* 2.2).

VII. (7) The Jews neither wanted to corrupt the sources nor could have done so. They did not want to, because, if they had wanted to corrupt any part, they would certainly have weakened the oracles which speak of Christ and confirm the Christian faith. Who indeed would believe that if, as is supposed, they did it from hatred of Christians, they would falsify the passages from which nothing against Christians can be drawn, and leave unchanged those in which Christians place the foundation for the triumph of the truth of the gospel? But this is exactly how the matter stands. The passages said to have been weakened by the Jews are little or no problem for Christians, while the most striking oracles concerning Christ remain unchanged, and are much plainer and more specific in Hebrew than in the translations, as has been pointed out by Jerome (epistle 74, to Marcellus), John Isaac (*Against Lindanus* 2), and Andradius in his defense of the Council of Trent, chapter 2. That they could not have done it no matter how badly they wanted to is shown not only by the large number of copies but also by the vigilance of Christians, not all of whose copies could the Jews have corrupted, and by the provident wisdom of God, who, if he will not permit one jot or tittle of the law to perish until all is fulfilled (Matt. 5:18), will be much less willing for the body of heavenly doctrine to be weakened by the Jews, and for us to be deprived of this treasure; rather, as Bellarmine well remarks, "for this purpose he willed to scatter the Jews throughout the world, and to disseminate the books of the law and the prophets, that, unwillingly, they might bear witness to our Christian truth" (*De Verbo Dei* 2.2 argument 5) .... and Augustine calls the Jews "a book-preserving people, carrying the law and the prophets; they used to carry the codices as a servant, that they might lose by carrying, and others gain by reading; they indeed serve us; the Jews were like book carriers and librarians, who by their efforts carried the codices for us," and again, "in their hearts, enemies; in their books, witnesses."

VIII. Although various small changes (*corruptulae*) may have come into the Hebrew codices through the carelessness of copyists or the ravages of time, they would not therefore cease to be the canon of faith and conduct. For these represent matters of small importance, not connected with faith and conduct, which Bellarmine himself admits, and therefore he denies that they affect the integrity of Scripture (*De Verbo Dei* 2.2); and moreover they are not found in every manuscript, and are not such as cannot readily be corrected from Scripture itself and the comparison of different copies.

IX. The hatred of Jews for Christians could be a remote cause for the corruption of Scripture, but one that could be impeded by a greater cause, namely, the providence of God, who envisioned a sure rule of faith for Christians no less than for Jews, one deduced from the indubitable foundations of the gospel, which could not be done if he allowed the sources to be corrupt.

X. The difference between the Septuagint and the original text does not imply that the text is corrupt, but rather that the translation is faulty, as Jerome already recognized in his day (in his prefaces to Deuteronomy and Chronicles, and in his letter to Sunias and Fretellas). Bellarmine says (*De Verbo Dei* 2.6) that [the Septuagint] is so corrupt and faulty that it seems altogether a different work, so that it is not safe today to emend the Hebrew or Latin text [of the Old Testament] from a Greek manuscript.

XI. So far is it from true that the *Keri* and *Kethib* divergencies, which are commonly regarded as 848 in number, corrupt the text, that rather they show the variant readings of different copies, by which all corruption by innovators is prevented. The *chasir* and *jothar*, which indicate a grammatical deficiency or superfluity, belong to the same category and make evident the superstition with which the Masoretes cared for the text.[2]

XII. The *tikkun sopherim* or "corrections of the scribes," of which there are only eighteen, do not imply any corruption of the text. Had there been any, Christ, if they were made before his time, or the orthodox fathers if they were

2. The second pair of Hebrew words can be found on lists of Masoretic terms, but does not seem too much used today by Christian scholars.

made later, would not have allowed them to pass without rebuke. Nor are they necessarily corrections, as is evident to the reader, but stylistic improvements, and changes not so much of meaning as of words. They were made either by the men of the Great Synagogue, one of whom, Ezra, who, after the return from the Babylonian captivity, restored to integrity the scattered and damaged copies of the sacred books, and arranged them as we now have them, was inspired by God, as we have already mentioned in the proper place,[3] or else by the authors themselves, who, after the custom of orators, edited what they had said. But the very content declares them to be of small moment, for the meaning is not lost even if the words are retained as spoken.

XIII. The similarity of some letters can indeed have resulted in errors appearing in some codices because of copyists' carelessness, but this was not universal, for they could easily be corrected from others, especially because of the thoroughness of the Masoretes, who counted not only all the words, but also the letters that were in the text.

XIV. So far it is from truth that the Masoretes' work suggests corruption of the sources, that, on the contrary, it was undertaken to prevent errors, so that in days to come not a single letter could be changed or dropped out.

XV. Although in Romans 10:18 the apostle writes "sound" for the "line" of Psalm 19:5 [4], it does not follow that the Hebrew text is corrupt and that "their line" was substituted for "their sound" or "voice." For *qav* means not only an extended or perpendicular line, but also a written line, or letter, by which young children are taught, as in Isaiah 28:10 the ignorant childishness of the Israelite people is shown when they are said to be taught like children "precept after precept, line after line." So the psalmist says,

3. Question 7, paragraph 12.

"Day teaches day, and one night shows forth knowledge to another." "Voice" (φθόγγος), which signifies not only the sound but the writing of the letter, renders this word [*qav*] well, just as we call diphthongs and vowels written. Moreover, Paul does not quote this verse exactly, but applies it in a figurative manner to the preaching of the gospel by the apostles, following the meaning rather than the words.

XVI. Corruption of the meaning is one thing; corruption of interpretation is another. The Jews have been able to corrupt the interpretation of Isaiah 9:6 when the words "and he shall call his name" are referred to the father who calls, not to the son who is called, but they have not corrupted the words themselves. Whether they are rendered as active or passive makes no difference, since according to Hebrew idiom a future active without subject often has a passive meaning, and so the words, impersonally in the third person, although active, can be understood as passive. So the Hebrew reading "and he shall call his name" has not been changed, but the subject must be supplied— not "God the Father," as the Jews take it, but "everyone," that is, all believers, shall call his (Christ's) name. To make this more plain, it is translated "his name shall be called." Likewise Jeremiah 23:6 has been somewhat corrupted in interpretation but not in the words, which are correctly translated either with a singular "he shall call him," as the seventy rendered it, as if the words referred to the nominative preceding "Israel and Judah," or with a plural, "they shall call him," as Pagninus, Vatable, and Arias Montanus render it, following the Chaldean, Syriac, Arabic, and the Vulgate. Jerome uses both renderings, and none of the Fathers called this passage corrupt.

XVII. Since three Targums understand "Shiloh" in Genesis 49:10 as "Messiah," it is clear that the Jews have not corrupted the passage in order to prove that the Messiah has not yet come. Moreover, this word *Shiloh*, which in the

Talmud is attributed to the Messiah, refutes the Jews and points to Christ no less than "Shiloh" [with final hard "h" rather than soft] which is asserted to have been the original, whether it be derived from "son" or from "peaceful," or, which seems preferable, and the Septuagint follows, a [Hebrew] phrase meaning "whose is the kingly authority." There is a similar phrase in Ezekiel 21:32 [27].[4]

XVIII. Zechariah 9:9 is not corrupt when it says that the Messiah is to be a king who is just and to be saved, for the word can be understood either as passive, meaning that Christ would be saved from death (Heb. 5:7), or would save himself (Isa. 63:3[5]); or as a deponent form used actively, which is common among the Hebrews, and this would be a participle meaning "liberator" or "savior."

XIX. Although in Exodus 12:40 the sojourn of the children of Israel in Egypt is said to have been of 430 years, which cannot be understood of the period of time spent in Egypt, which was 215 years, but of the time spent both in Canaan and in Egypt, as the Samaritan and the Greek explain the passage, the Hebrew ought not to be regarded as corrupt but as synechdoche, which remembers only the Egyptian period, because it was the principal exile of the Israelites, by naming the whole from the more important part.

XX. In Psalm 15 [14] no verses have been omitted [from the present Hebrew text], for what is quoted in Romans 3:11 – 12 was not taken by the apostle from there, but from many psalms put together, for example, Psalms 5, 11, 26, 36, and 140, and from Isaiah 59, as Jerome teaches in his commentary on Isaiah (book 16).

XXI. I Corinthians 15:47 is not corrupt in the Greek text, but in the Vulgate, which omits the word *Lord*, which here means Christ, as he is not a mere man but the Lord Jehovah, and so the antithesis between the first and second

---

4. The verse citation follows the Hebrew and the Septuagint.

Adam is much stronger: "the first man is of the earth, earthy, but the second man is the Lord from heaven."

XXII. Although the doxology of Matthew 6:13, in the conclusion of the Lord's Prayer, is not found in Luke 11, nor in many manuscripts, it does not follow that this text is corrupt, because the Lord could have taught the same form of prayer twice; once without the doxology, and then again, with it added, for the general public. Nor is it impossible for one Gospel to leave out what another includes, for no necessity makes each one include everything; Matthew 6:33 reads, "Seek the kingdom of God and his righteousness," but Luke 6:31 has only, "Seek the kingdom of God."[5] What Luke omits ought therefore not to be eliminated, but supplied from Matthew, since both are inspired, especially because this passage is found in all the Greek manuscripts of Matthew, as Erasmus and Bellarmine recognize.

XXIII. Although in a number of manuscripts Romans 12:11 reads "serving the time," this is not the case with all; indeed Franciscus Lucas says he has seen six which read "Lord." Beza says this is the reading of a number of the best, and Dominic a Soto states that that reading is now general, both in Greek and Latin.[6]

XXIV. It is certain that all Greek manuscripts differ from the Latin in I John 4:3, for the Greek has "every spirit that does not confess that Jesus has come in the flesh," but the Latin, "every spirit that takes Jesus apart (*solvit*)." It does not follow that the sources are corrupt, for the Greek reading is more worthy (*augustior*), and much more specific against Nestorius and Eutyches.

XXV. Corruption is one thing; a variant reading is another. We admit that there are a number of variant readings com-

---

5. The reference should be Luke 12:31.

6. This is the reading of the Clementine Vulgate, and the contemporary Latin texts of Nestle and Bover.

ing from the collation of various manuscripts, but we deny that there is a universal corruption.

XXVI. It is one thing to speak of the effort of heretics to corrupt certain manuscripts. We readily concede this. The complaints of the Fathers, for example, Irenaeus with regard to Marcion, Origen on Romans 16:13, and Theodoret with regard to Tatian are relevant to this. But success, or complete and universal corruption, is another matter. This we deny, both because of the providence of God, who did not allow them to do what they planned, and because of the diligence of the orthodox fathers, who, having various manuscripts in their possession, were faithful in keeping them free from corruption.

The Authentic Version
of Scripture

QUESTION **11**

Arc the Hebrew version of the Old Testament and the Greek of the New the only authentic ones? (Affirmative, against the Roman Catholics)

I. Some versions of Scripture are original and primary, originally prepared by the authors; others are secondary, versions in other languages into which it has been translated. No one denies that the Hebrew of the Old Testament and the Greek of the New are original and first written, but there is a controversy between us and the Roman Catholics as to whether both are authentic, and deserve in themselves both faith and authority, and whether all other versions are to be tested by them.

II. Some Roman Catholics—Sixtus Senensis, Driedo, Andradius, and others—do justice to the sources by affirming their purity, as seen above, and, on account of their purity, ascribing authenticity to them, so that all versions, including even the Vulgate, may be corrected from them. But more of them do not, and hold that there is no certainty about the substance of the Hebrew, either for appeal to the sources in controversies over faith, or for correcting the Vulgate from it; for example, Stapleton, Cano, Lindanus, and others who contend for the corruption of the sources. This teaching is taken from the decree of the Council of

Trent, session 4, which said: "Let the Latin Vulgate version be held authoritative for public reading, disputation, preaching, and exposition, in the sense that no one dare reject it for any reason." It is granted that many Roman Catholics, who are ashamed of this decree, try to construe it in another sense, as if the council had said nothing against the authenticity of the original text, and had not given the Vulgate precedence over the sources, but had only chosen one out of the Latin versions which were in circulation, which it declared superior to the others, as Bellarmine says (*De Verbo Dei* 2.10), which is also the opinion of Andradius, Salmeron, Serarius, and others. That this is a distortion of the decree of the Synod Bannes rightly argues, and it can easily be seen from the words of the council itself. For if it is to be held as authoritative, and no one is to dare reject it for any reason, is it not equated with the sources, and indeed made superior to them? If it differs from the sources it will not be brought into harmony with them, but rather they made to agree with it. So Mariana concludes that after the promulgation of [the decrees of the] Council of Trent "the Greek and Hebrew have fallen with one blow." But our teaching is that only the Hebrew of the Old Testament and the Greek of the New have been and are authentic[1] in the sense that all controversies concerning faith and religion, and all versions, are to be tested and examined by them.

III. An authentic writing is one with regard to which all factors together produce confidence, and to which complete trust should be given in its field, from which it is evident both that it must come from the author whose name it bears, and that everything in it must be written as

1. The word *authenticus* means, for Turretin, both "genuine" and "authoritative." As he has shown, the two words, as applied to the Bible, have virtually the same meaning in his theology. In translating, it has not been advisable to consistently use any one English word for this term.

he wanted it written. Such a writing can be authentic in either of two senses—primary and original and secondary and derivative. The primary sense applies to what bears its own authentication, which proves itself by itself, and which is believed and clearly should be believed on its own showing (*ob seipsum*). In this category are the original copies of royal edicts, of the decrees of magistrates, wills, contracts, and anything else actually written by the author. In the secondary group are all copies accurately and faithfully made by qualified (*idoneus*) persons, such as the functionaries appointed and authorized by public authority to copy the edicts of princes and other public documents, or the various honest and faithful scribes and copyists of books and other writings. In the first sense only the "autographs" of Moses, the prophets and the apostles are authentic, but in the second sense faithful and accurate copies are also.

IV. Furthermore, the authority of such authentic writing has two aspects: one rests on the substance of the matter with which it deals (*in rebus ipsis de quibus id agitur*), and concerns the people to whom the writing is directed; the other concerns the word itself and the writing and applies to the copies and translations made from it, and receives all its authority (*ius*) from the original, so that it should be compared to that authentic writing and corrected if there is any difference. The first kind of authority (*authoritas*) may be greater or less, depending on the authority of him by whom the writing was issued, and whether he has more or less authority (*imperium*) over the people to whom he addresses it. With the Holy Scripture, authority is found to the greatest degree, such as cannot reside in any other writing, since we ought simply to obey God, and be obedient to everything which he has, in his most holy authentic written Word, required either to be believed or to be done, on account of that supreme authority which he holds over mankind, as over all creation, and that supreme truth and wisdom which reside in him. But the second kind of authority consists in this, that faithful and accurate copies, not less than autographs, are norms for all other copies of his writing and for translations. If any discrepancy is found in these, whether it conflicts with the originals or the true copies, they are not worthy of the name "authentic," and must be rejected as false and corrupted, and there is no other reason for this rejection except the discrepancy. We wrote above, in question 4, about the first kind of authority. Here we discuss the second, which is found in the authentic version (*editio*).

V. Finally, authenticity can be seen in two ways: materially, with regard to the teaching (*res enunciata*), or formally, with regard to the words and the methods (*modus enunciandi*). It is not a question here of the first—we do not deny this authenticity to the versions when they agree with the sources—but only of the second, which belongs only to the sources.

VI. The reasons are (1) only the sources are inspired both in substance and in wording (II Tim. 3:16); therefore only they can be authentic. For what men of God wrote they wrote guided by the Holy Spirit (II Peter 1:21), who, lest they fall into error, determined (*dictavit*) not only the substance but also the words, which cannot be said of any translation (*versio*). (2) They are the norm and rule by which all versions are to be tested, as the ectype must be referred to the archetype and a brook is recognized from its source. The canon of Gratian based on Augustine reads: "That the trustworthiness of the old books be tested from the Hebrew manuscripts; thus the truth of the Greek of the new falls short of the norm." Much is presented by Jerome in this matter as he argues for the authority of the Hebrew text: see his letter 102 to Marcellus and letters to Vitalus, and to Sunias and Fretellas. (3) These texts (*editiones*) have been held as authentic from the beginning, and were always so held by Jews and Christians, for many centuries after Christ, and no reason can be given why they should now cease to be authentic. For the reasons that have been suggested to support the concept of corruption not only assume what should be proved but also have been refuted by us.

VII. (4) If the Hebrew of the Old Testament and the Greek of the New are not authentic, there is no authentic version; no other has divine witness to its authenticity. If there is no authentic Word of God in the church, there will be no end of strife, for there will be no assured rule of faith and conduct to which all must agree, and Scripture will be like a wax nose, or a law of Lesbos interpreted in accordance with private judgment. (5) Our adversaries admit that in some cases it is necessary to refer to the sources. Bellarmine gives the following cases:[2] (a) when there seems to be a copyist's error in the Latin manuscripts; (b) when there are variant readings, so that it is impossible to be sure which is right; (c) when there is ambiguity either in the words or the content; (d) when the force and connotation of the [Latin] words are not explicit enough (*De Verbo Dei* 2.11). This could not be valid unless the sources were authentic. Arias Montanus, in his preface to the Bible,[3] shows that errors in the versions cannot be corrected except from the truth of the original language. Vives lays it down as certain and beyond doubt that recourse must be had to the sources. Salmeron, Bonfrerius, Masius, Muisius, Jansen and his followers, and others who presently appeal to the sources have the same conviction.[4]

2. The clauses indicated by a, b, c, and d are noted by a second series of Arabic numerals in the original. I have made the change in accordance with contemporary practice in outlining.

3. The Antwerp Polyglot (1572).

4. At this point, Turretin quotes no Protestant authority, but contents himself with the "testimony of adversaries."

VIII. The variant readings that occur in Scripture do not detract from its authenticity, because they are easily recognized and understood, partly by the context (*cohaerentia textus*), and partly by collation of the better manuscripts; many are of such nature that, although they differ, yet they agree in meaning (*licet diversae non male tamen eidem textui conveniant*).

IX. Although a number of controversies have arisen from the Hebrew and Greek sources, it does not follow that they cannot be authentic, because if they were not, there would be no authentic version of the Bible whatsoever to which appeal could be made; there is no language which would not offer much opportunity for argumentative disputation. Moreover, [controversy] is not the fault of the sources but of those who abuse the sources, either not understanding them or twisting them to their own opinions, and stubbornly sticking to the same.

X. The statement that the Hebrew manuscripts of the Old Testament and the Greek of the New have become defective is false, and the passages which are offered in proof of this by our adversaries cannot demonstrate it. Not the pericope of adultery (John 8), which, although it is lacking in the Syriac, is found in all the Greek manuscripts. Not the saying in I John 5:7, although formerly some called it into question, and heretics do so today. All the Greek witnesses (*exemplaria*) have it, as Sixtus Senensis recognizes: "The words always were of unquestioned truth, and are read in all Greek manuscripts from the time of the apostles themselves."[5] Not Mark 16, which was lacking in a number of manuscripts in Jerome's time, as he admits, but now is found in all, and also in the Syriac, and is

5. In a disputation *De tribus testibus coelestibus* (*Opera*, vol. 4), Turretin discusses I John 5:7 in detail, and identifies the "heretics" as Socinians.

clearly necessary to complete the account of Christ's resurrection.

XI. It is useless for our adversaries to use the newness of the vowel points in the Hebrew manuscripts as a means of overcoming their authenticity, as if the points were merely a human innovation made by the Masoretes, depending therefore not on divine and infallible authority, but on human, and therefore subject to change by human decision, without risk, so that the meaning of the text remains forever uncertain and ambiguous. They can be answered in a number of ways. (1) Bellarmine will give this reply on our behalf: "The errors which arise on account of the addition of the points do not affect truth, because the points have been added externally, and do not change the text" (*De Verbo Dei* 2.2). (2) On this hypothesis, not only does assurance concerning the original text leave us, but also assurance concerning the Vulgate, which was prepared from that source, unless it can be shown that the first author of that version, whether Jerome or somebody else, received directly from the Spirit the necessary revelation concerning the vowels, which otherwise surely came from the tradition of the Jews. If that was uncertain, all the authority of the sacred text totters.

XII. (3) Even if the points were added at a late date, as these who date their origin from the Masoretes of Tiberias claim, it does not follow that they are merely a human device, depending only on human judgment, which indeed, if it be assumed, considerably weakens the authority of the Hebrew manuscript. For the pointing, in the opinion of those who hold this hypothesis, is not supposed to have been done according to the judgment of the rabbis, but according to the analogy of Scripture, the nature (*genius*) of the sacred language, and the meaning that had long been accepted by the Jews, so that even if the points were not, as on this hypothesis, part of the original with regard to their shape, it cannot be denied that they always were part of it with regard to sound and value, or power. Otherwise, since vowels are the souls of consonants, the text would always have been ambiguous; indeed no clear meaning of the word would be possible unless [the vowels] were as old as the consonants, as Prideaux in his twelfth lecture on the antiquity of the points soundly observes: "That the points and accents were part of the original in respect to sound and value no one denies: [the question] only concerns the marks and characters." And again, "the vowels were as old as the consonants with regard to underlying quality (*vis*) and sound, although the dots and marks which are now employed had not then appeared." Indeed it is hardly possible to doubt that the vowels, if not with the same marks that are now written, were nevertheless indicated by some marks in place of the points, in order that the sure and unchanging message (*sensus*) of the Holy Spirit, which otherwise, depending merely on human learning and memory, could easily have been forgotten, or corrupted, might be retained. [This could have been done,] as some suppose, by the letters *aleph*, *waw*, and *yodh*, which are therefore called "the mothers of speech." Such is the opinion of the learned [Brian] Walton, who says, "By usage and the tradition of the elders, the true reading and pronounciation had been preserved by means of the three letters *aleph*, *waw*, and *yodh* which are called mothers of speech and which served in place of vowels before the introduction of the points" (*Prolegomena to the* [London] *Polyglot* 7).

XIII. (4) Our adversaries arbitrarily assume what requires proof, that points are a modern and human addition, a conclusion with which a great many Jews, notably Eli Levi, who lived a century ago, disagreed, in which they were followed by many highly regarded philologists (*grammatici*) and theologians, both Protestant and Catholic—Junius, Illyricus, Reuchlin, Münster, Cevalerius, Pagninus, M. Marinus, Polanus, Deodatus, Broughton, Muisius, Taylor, Booth, Lightfoot, and most theologians since them. The whole case seems to have been settled by the Buxtorfs, father and son, the first in his *Tiberias*, the second in that most thorough work with which he refuted *Arcanum punctationis revelatum*.[6] It would not be difficult to support this position by a number of considerations, if we should now turn our attention to it, but since the question is one of philology rather than of theology we do not care to make it our battle. It is enough to have it understood that to us the teaching that regards the points as of divine origin has always seemed truer and safer, for the support of the authenticity of the original text whole and complete against heretics, and the establishing of a sure and changeless principle of faith, whether [the points] come from Moses or from Ezra, the leader of the Great Synagogue, and so it is useless for our adversaries to seek to question the authority of the Hebrew manuscripts on the ground of the newness of the points.[7]

6. A work by Louis Cappel of the Reformed academy of Saumur, France, published as an appendix to his *Commentarii et notae critici in Vetus Testamentum*, Leiden, 1624. The younger Buxtorf's reply, *Tractatus de punctorum . . . origine antiquitate et authoritate*, had appeared in Basel in 1648. A new edition of the *Arcanum* was printed in Amsterdam in 1689, a year after Turretin's work appeared in Geneva, indicating that the question was still under discussion, but it will be noted that Turretin can marshal an impressive amount of scholarly opinion for his conclusions. See also the following question.

7. The principle of Turretin's argument is that the authority of Scripture has been established on firm grounds, and that therefore intellectual puzzles do not threaten it. This conclusion regarding the vowel points had, with his reluctant consent, been made part of the confession of faith, largely through the influence of J. H. Heidegger of Zurich, in the short-lived "Helvetic Consensus Formula" (1675), which was adopted in Switzerland only, and remained in force for about a generation.

The Authenticity
of the Hebrew Text

QUESTION **12**

Is the present Hebrew text authentic and inspired both as to content and as to words, so that all versions are to be tested by its norm, and corrected if they differ? Or can the text which it offers, if judged to be less desirable, be rejected, and corrected, and brought into agreement with a more acceptable one, either by comparison with the old translations, or by one's own judgment and critical ability?

I. Since the authenticity of the sacred text is the primary foundation of the faith, nothing should take precedence among all believers over its preservation inviolate against all attacks, whether they reject it altogether or weaken it in any way. For this purpose the preceding controversy with the Catholics was undertaken, and the present question, in which we turn to an examination of the opinions of the reverend and learned Louis Cappel, deals with the same issue. Just as he began strongly arguing the newness of the vowel points, as a recent innovation of the Masoretes and hence the result of human effort and study, in his work *Arcanum punctationis revelatum*, so in his *Critica sacra* he tries earnestly to show that we are not so bound to the present reading of the Hebrew text as to make it improper often to depart from it whenever we can find a better and more appropriate reading either by comparison with the old translations, or by the power of right reason, or by one's own judgment and critical ability. We do not undertake this controversy in any unfriendly spirit, as if we sought to detract from the reputation of a man who in other ways deserves esteem from the church of God. We only wish to uphold the conviction always up to now maintained in our churches concerning the inviolate authenticity of the sacred text, against those who are trying to adopt these "significant opinions"[1] and new hypotheses, or who speak of them as inconsequential matters that are of no concern to the faith, or at least of very little.[2]

II. His teaching amounts to this: (1) because the points are a human addition, they may, when the need is postulated, be changed and others substituted, whenever the meaning which they yield is false or absurd. (2) Not only may the pointing be changed, but also the substantial text, but there is more freedom with regard to the points, because the Masoretes often decided on them in accordance with their own private judgment, to which we ought not to be bound. (3) If, by use of ancient translations, whether Greek, Aramaic, or Latin, a meaning of the versions can be established that is equally good and appropriate, or superior to our Hebrew manuscripts, it is permissible to change the reading, and follow the other. (4) Not only by comparison with the old translations can this be done, but also, if we are able to show a weakness in the present reading, and that it is either meaningless, or absurd or false, and are able to find a clearer or more suitable meaning through another more appropriate reading, whether by the power of sound reason, or the natural faculty of thinking and discussing, or by conjecture, then it is per-

1. κυρίας *istas* δόξας, a term of Epicurean origin, perhaps used pejoratively.

2. The work of Cappel, a distinguished professor at Saumur, was in many ways an anticipation of nineteenth-century higher criticism. Turretin realized that such opinions, expressed by a respected Protestant theologian, had far-reaching consequences. For the movement, see Brian G. Armstrong, *Calvinism and the Amyraut Heresy: Protestant Scholasticism and Humanism in Seventeenth-Century France* (Madison: University of Wisconsin Press, 1969).

missible to strike out the present Hebrew text, and sub-
stitute the other. That this is his teaching can be known
from various passages, and especially from this one: "It is
therefore permissible, if any reading different from the
present Hebrew text, either with regard to consonants or
letters, or to words and whole sentences, has any equally
appropriate meaning, for it to be held more genuine, sound,
and complete, wherever it was found, whether in the Septuagint, or the Aramaic Targums, or Aquila, or Symmachus,
Theodotion, or Jerome the translator of the Vulgate, and
therefore it is to be followed and accepted rather than the
existing Masoretic text," a statement which he often ex-
presses in other places.

III. To support this opinion, he makes another hypothesis, namely, that the Hebrew manuscripts which the seventy and other translators used were different from the
present ones, which he disparagingly calls Masoretic and
Jewish, and that the differences between the old translations and the present Hebrew text are variant readings of
the Hebrew text, except perhaps some which arose from
the mistakes of translators who either did not know the
meaning of the Hebrew word or did not pay enough attention. So he denies that our present Hebrew Bible can
be regarded as the source, but accepts it only as one form
of the text, and holds that the true and genuine authentic
original text must be established at length by comparison
of the old versions. So he distinguishes between the Hebrew text in itself and the present Masoretic text. The latter
is to be found in all copies which exist today, both among
Jews and among Christians; the former can be put together
by comparing the present text and the old translations,
which in some cases he not only regards as of equal value
to the present [Hebrew], but he also clearly regards them
as superior, since he often holds that the reading they give,
as more appropriate and true, is to be followed in prefer-

ence to that of the present [Hebrew]. "Not only if the reading of the Septuagint is better than the present [Hebrew],
but if equally good and appropriate, then, because older
and of equal goodness in language and meaning, it should
be preferred, because of the version's age" (*Apologia contra
Bootium*, p. 54). And again, "The authority of Septuagint
manuscripts is greater than that of the present [Hebrew],
not only in those places where it gives a more appropriate
meaning, but also where it provides one equally good and
appropriate, and this because of its greater age. The same
can and should be said concerning all codices of old
translators."

IV. But the accepted and usual opinion of our churches
is very different, namely, not recognizing [as authoritative]
any text except the present Hebrew, to which, as a touch-
stone, all versions ancient and modern must be subjected,
and corrected if they differ, while it cannot be emended
from them. Although they hold that individual manuscripts can and should be compared to one another, in
order that variant readings, originating in the carelessness
of copyists or librarians, can be discovered and the errors
in these and other manuscripts corrected, and do not
deny that comparison with the old translations is useful
for the understanding of the true meaning, yet they deny
that the old translations are even of equal, much less of
superior, value to the original text, to the extent that the
meaning which they offer, and which seems more appropriate to us, can be accepted, and another, which comes
from existing [Hebrew] text, be rejected.

V. That always, from the beginning, this was the conviction (*mens*) of all Protestants is clearer than the light of
noon, and the controversy over the authentic text against
the Roman Catholics shows this adequately. Nor can the
learned man against whom we argue deny it. In his *Critica
sacra*, book 1, chapter 1, he says, "The first and old Prot-

estants said that everything must be examined and corrected on the basis of the Hebrew text, which they called the purest source." Sixtinus Amama confirms this in his much-praised book (1:3) after giving his own opinion on this question; he says, "We conclude that all translations, whether ancient or modern, with no exception, are to be tested by it (namely, the Hebrew text)"; "it is the norm, rule, and canon of all translations." And in chapter 4: "Therefore no translation, of whatever kind it may be, can be on a par with the Hebrew text, much less superior to it. This Protestants hold concerning all versions ancient or modern."

VI. From the above the status of this question can easily be seen. It is not a question whether versions may be compared with one another, and with the original, to discover the true meaning. But [the question is] whether it is permissible to give equal or greater weight to a reading taken from them, which seems more appropriate for substitution in place of the present reading, when, in our opinion, that gives either no meaning, or a false and absurd one. It is not a question whether there are differences between the present text and the old translations, but whether these differences are to be understood as variant readings of the Hebrew, so that no authentic text can be recognized except that which results from the comparison of the existing text with the old translations. Finally, it is not a question whether in the study and comparison of one codex with another, whether manuscripts or printed editions, we can use our judgment, and our ratiocinative faculty, to discover probabilities, and decide which reading is better or more appropriate, but whether it is permissible to make critical conjectures about the sacred text no less than about secular writers, to change letters and points and even words, when the meaning of the existing [Hebrew] text does not seem appropriate to us, which the learned man maintains; we deny it.

VII. The reasons are (1) from this hypothesis it follows that there is no authentic text in which faith can totally put its trust, for this would either be the existing Hebrew text or other codices which the old translators used. But on this hypothesis the existing text is merely one of several forms, and its reading can be regarded as the authentic Hebrew source only where there is no difference between it and the old translations, as the learned man says in his *apologia* against Booth, page 17. As for the other codices used by the ancient translators—besides the fact that it is arbitrarily assumed that they were different from the present text, which is his first fallacy, as will be shown later— if we grant that there were such, they cannot now be the basis of faith, for they cannot be found, and no longer exist except in that translation, which, because it is human and fallible, cannot yield an authentic text. Finally, who could make anyone believe that the seventy followed their Hebrew text with absolute exactness, and that the present Greek text is exactly the one they produced?

VIII. (2) [a][3] If all the discrepancies between the old versions and the present Hebrew text were variant readings of Hebrew manuscripts different from ours, which the translators used, why was there no mention of such manuscripts among the patristic writers, and no trace among the Hebrews, who for many centuries have been so zealous in finding and correcting the smallest variant, as the collections of variants by Ben Asher and Ben Naphtali, Eastern and Western, give evidence? Who could believe that the variants of the least significance would have been recorded, and that those now found on the basis of the old translations had so fully disappeared that no memory of them survived? Since there were so many copies, it is in-

3. The letters in brackets have been substituted for a confusing second series of Arabic numerals in the text.

deed a marvel that none have survived. [b] It is arbitrary to assume that there is no cause for these discrepancies, except differences in the codices, when others are far more certain [to have been present]. On that assumption one would conclude, wrongly, that for the contemporary versions the translators used different texts, although none except the present one exists, for there are innumerable differences among the translations. Who does not realize that often they could have rendered the meaning rather than the words, as Jerome often notes concerning the seventy? Finally, some discrepancies could have arisen from [the translators'] ignorance or carelessness, because they did not pay enough attention to the words, and often, therefore, could have confused similar letters and words, even without a variant text, as Jerome often accuses them. [c] They would have assumed presumptuous liberties if they read one thing in their manuscripts, and boldly wrote something else, which did not agree with the meaning and context of the Hebrew, and preferred, with a capricious change, to follow the meaning that they thought better. [d] The various old versions are no longer in their original state, but are corrupted and changed remarkably, as is especially true of the Septuagint and the Vulgate. [e] The negligence or ignorance of the copyists could have introduced into the versions many corruptions, which therefore did not originate in variant readings.

IX. (3) [On this hypothesis] the various versions are of the same significance as the original text, for if, in all cases of divergence, the old translations are no more to be subjected to the text than it to them, but both are subjected to a common canon of more appropriate meaning, so that the reading with the greater appropriateness of meaning will survive, whether it be found in the Hebrew text or in one or another of those translations, then the Hebrew text will hold no authority over the old translation except when it is found to have greater appropriateness of meaning, and indeed it will often be subordinated to the translations, when its reading is less esteemed than another.

x. (4) If we are not bound to the present Hebrew text, but the true authentic reading must be sought partly by comparison with the old translations, and partly by our own judgment and critical ability, so that there is no canon of authentic reading other than what seems to us more appropriate, then the determination of the authentic reading will be the work of reason and of human judgment (*arbitrium*),[4] not of the Holy Spirit. Human reason will be enthroned, and, in the Socinian manner, regarded as norm and principle of faith.

xi. (5) If conjectures can be made about the sacred text, even when the Hebrew agrees with the versions, as the learned man argues (*Critica sacra* 6.8 par. 17), there can no longer be any assurance concerning the authenticity of the sacred text, but everything will be made doubtful and uncertain, and the sacred text subjected to the judgment of every individual interpreter. Any prudent person will easily determine whether or not this will deprive it of all authority. It is useless to reply that conjectures are not to be accepted unless they depend on, and are demonstrated by, assured reasons and arguments, when the received reading yields either a false and absurd meaning, or a doubtful and confused one. For there will be no one who does not think that he can give reasons for his conjecture, and who cannot make a case for the falsity and absurdity of the reading which he wants to reject. Who can be a

4. *Arbitrium*, which I have rendered "judgment," also means "will," and was therefore a loaded, emotional term in Protestant theology. Turretin here shows great reluctance to see human faculties as the means used by the Holy Spirit. The insistence that only in direct ("supernatural") action should one look for the work of the Spirit suggests much of the controversy between Geneva and Saumur, on several issues.

judge of these conjectures, whether they are rightly and truly made? And without a judge there will be continual struggles and disputes among the commentators, since each one will contend for his opinion, and will not permit others to be preferred to it. If a place is allowed for conjectures in the study of the various codices, to find out which reading is better and more appropriate, new readings must continually be admitted, which depend on the authority of no accepted manuscript, but on private judgment, and which can be of no value, but will be of the greatest danger and the certain discredit of the Scriptures because of the enormous and rash presumption of mankind. Nor can the example of secular writers, who can be subjected to criticism without danger, be relevant here, as if sacred and secular criticism were the same, and there was not the greatest difference between a writing that is human and subject to error, and one that is divine and inspired, whose majesty should be sacrosanct, because it has been received with the veneration, preserved with the care, and approved with the widespread agreement, that the origins of its truth, and the certification of its source, deserve. What indeed will happen to this sacred volume if everyone is permitted to modify its style like a censor, and to offer criticism, just as with secular books?

XII. (6) If the existing Hebrew text is given no primacy over the old translations, so that it has no more authority than they, and indeed their readings are often to be preferred, when they seem to yield a more appropriate sense, then Protestants up to now have struggled in vain against the Roman Catholics when they affirmed the sole authority of the existing Hebrew text, above all versions ancient or modern; nor can they any longer insist against them that all versions and especially the Vulgate must be subjected to it and corrected by it, since the versions often are not only of equal value, but superior.

XIII. A variant reading is one thing; varying interpretation is another. Commentators may give various interpretations, but it does not follow that these are drawn from variant readings in the codices, rather than the other causes which we noted.

XIV. It is not necessary for the scribes[5] to have been infallible for there to have been no variants in the Hebrew codices; it was sufficient for providence so to guard the integrity of the authentic codices, that, although they could introduce various errors through ignorance or negligence, they either did not introduce them, or did not introduce them into all copies, or did not introduce them in such a way that they cannot be restored and corrected by comparison of the various codices with the Scripture itself.

XV. Although we say rightly (*bene*) that Scripture is made uncertain by diverse variant readings from different interpreters, based only on conjectures, it is not made uncertain simply by various interpretations, because the interpreters have interpreted one and the same text in different ways. Thus the meaning is made doubtful and uncertain, but not the reading of the words and phrases; but if various and uncertain readings and conjectures are assumed, it becomes more difficult to sustain assurance, because a double uncertainty—the text and meaning—has been introduced. In the first instance a sure foundation is postulated, on which the differing interpretations are based, but in the second case no sure foundation is postulated, but everything depends on human judgment and decision.

XVI. It is not necessary to show us the actual writing of Moses and the prophets, without any even minor discrepancy, in order that we may be bound to the existing text.

5. *Scribae*, capitalized, must mean the official Hebrew scribes, guardians of the sacred text. It is not Turretin's ordinary word for copyist.

For to uphold the exact conformity of our copies with the archetype, it is sufficient that both the words, without which there is no meaning, and letters, without which there are no words, be the same, nor could the scribes have written without these [words and letters], although some discrepancies in details and punctuation would be possible.

XVII. Although the learned man often declares that all versions must be examined and corrected on the basis of the authentic Hebrew text, which is to be given precedence over all translations, he cannot be freed from the charge that has been made against him—that he regards the old versions as of equal authority with the text, and sometimes as superior, because he does not mean the existing original text, which is in the hands of all, both Jews and Christians, but the Hebrew text in general, which he desires to put together from the existing text and from the text which he supposes that the old translators used, which, as said above, is affirmed without solid evidence. Up to now all the theologians who have discussed the Hebrew text and its authenticity have understood nothing else by it than the text now accepted.

XVIII. From the above, to add nothing more, it is clear enough how dangerous the learned man's hypotheses are, and with what reason our [theologians] everywhere have resisted the publication of his work, lest a future which they have foreseen—something harmful to the cause of God—come from it, and our adversaries be furnished with weapons against the authenticity of the sacred text, which, beyond all doubt, is not his intention.

XIX. If anyone wants more on this, let him consult the *Anticritica* of the famous Buxtorf, who opposes the *Critica* of this learned man, in which this whole discussion is fully and soundly set forth. Other great men also offer witness by which it can be known how much their opinions differ from the writings of this learned man. For instance, James

Ussher, the archbishop of Armagh, says, in his letter to Booth, that they contain a "very dangerous error." ... And Arnold Booth is of the same mind, in a letter to that venerable leader [Ussher], and in his *Vindicium*, in which he refers to [Cappel's] work as "a very evil writing. ..." But for us the witness of the great Andrew Rivet, a man of high repute throughout France and Holland, is enough. Although when he first read the learned man's *Arcanum* he was drawn to his opinion, later, having read Buxtorf's reply, he speaks very differently in a letter to him from the Hague dated 1645. ... Many who, although at first favorable to the learned man's hypotheses, afterward studied the question more carefully and read the arguments against his speculations by the famed Buxtorf and others, were not ashamed of abandoning their former opinion, and took a sounder position.[6]

6. I have omitted much of the quoted material with which the section closes. What is printed gives the substance of the whole, and shows that Turretin, writing in 1685, could find solid scholarly support for his conclusions. That he had to argue them against a distinguished French Protestant, at a time when French Protestantism had undergone a major crisis, was a historical complication of his dogmatic problem.

The Need of Translations

QUESTION **13** Are translations necessary, and what is their authority and use in the church?

I. There are two parts of this question: the first concerning the need for translations, and the second their authority. As to the first, although the wiser Roman Catholics recognize the need and value of translations, and have therefore prepared them in many languages, yet many of them, having lost their reason, condemn them as evil and dangerous; for example, Arbor says, "The translation of the sacred writings into the vulgar tongue is the sole origin of heresies," and Soto, Harding, Bayle, and many of the order of Loyola agree—against whom the Reformed uphold not only the value but also the need of translations, and prove it by a number of arguments.

II. (1) Reading of, and reflection upon, Scripture is required (*praecepta*) of people of all languages. Therefore its translation into the vernacular is necessary, for, since mankind is divided into many linguistic groups, and not everyone is acquainted with the two languages in which it was first given, it cannot be understood by such unless translated; therefore [the Scripture] would say nothing at all, or what no one understands. But [by translations] the marvelous grace of God has brought it about that the difference of languages, which formerly was the sign of his wrath, now is an evidence of heavenly blessing; that which was first used for the destruction of Babel is now employed in the construction of the mystical Zion.

III. (2) The gospel is to be preached in all languages; therefore it can and should be translated into all. This is a logical deduction from the preached word to the written, because the significance (*ratio*) is the same, and the reasons that led the apostles to preach in the vernacular make plain the need of translations. Although the apostles wrote only in one language, it does not follow that Scripture cannot be translated into others, for there is one rule (*ratio*) for the sources, another for the translations: the sources should have been written in one language, and so the apostles, as teachers of the universal church, should have written only in the universal and most common language, which at that time was Greek, just as the Old Testament, which was intended for the Jews, was written in Hebrew, their vernacular. But where Greek has passed out of use, there is need of translation for the proclamation of the gospel.

IV. (3) It is certain that both Eastern and Western churches had their translations, and worshiped in the language of the people as a sacred language, as is evident from their liturgies. Why should not the same thing be done today, since there is the same need and reason for teaching the people? When the two memorable dispersions of the Israelites, one among the Chaldeans and the other among the Greeks, took place, and God's people by using the local language almost forgot Hebrew, the Chaldean Targum or paraphrase, and later the Greek translation, were made for the sake of the uneducated. There were several Targums. The first was the Chaldean paraphrase of Jonathan the son of Uziel, a disciple of Hillel, contemporary of Simeon, who lived forty years before Christ. When he saw that true Hebrew was little by little falling into disuse, he prepared a Chaldean version, lest the people be denied so great a treasure; we have this version of the former and latter prophets. To this Onkelos, who lived after Christ and was a contemporary of Gamaliel, added a translation of the Pentateuch. There is also a paraphrase of the Hagiographa, but no real knowledge of its author. There are also Syriac, Arabic, Persian, and Ethiopic versions, but they are less used and less well known.[1] For the New Testament, there is a Syriac translation, which is believed to be the oldest, and which is ascribed by some to the church of Antioch.

V. Greek translations of the Old Testament, of which there are also many, followed these. The first and most famous is the Septuagint, which was made under Ptolemy Philadelphus of Egypt about three hundred years before Christ. The second is that of Aquila of Pontus, under the emperor Hadrian, about A.D. 137. He was first of the Greek religion, then a Christian; when the church was disturbed by foolish fanaticism over astrology he defected to the Jews because of the strife of Christians, and translated the Old Testament in order to corrupt the oracles about Christ. The third was by Theodotion, who lived under Commodus, about A.D. 184, and was of the Pontic nation and the Marcionite faith. After becoming a Jew he prepared a new translation in which he followed the Septuagint as much as possible. The fourth was by Symmachus, who lived under the emperors Antoninus [Pius] and [Marcus] Aurelius, about A.D. 197.[2] He was at first a Samaritan, but became a Jew and translated the Old Testament to refute

1. The inclusion of the Targums is indicative of Turretin's concept of the church, or covenant people, as one through various phases of history, before and after Christ. The unity of revelation corresponds to a unity of God's people, and the behavior of pre-Christian Jews is an example of the behavior of the church.

2. This date, as well as the others in this paragraph, is given in Turretin's text. Turretin may have referred to the approximate date of Symmachus's death, although he does not say so.

the Samaritans. To these two others of unknown author-
ship were added: the Jericho version found in a jar near
Jericho in the time of Caracalla, about A.D. 220, and the
Nicopolitan version, found near Nicopolis in the time of
Alexander Severus, about 230. By bringing all of these together, Origen made his Tetrapla, Hexapla, and Octapla.
The Tetrapla contained four Greek versions in separate col-
umns—the Septuagint, Aquila, Symmachus, and Theodotion. In the Hexapla he added two Hebrew versions, one
in Hebrew letters and one in Greek. In the Octapla the two
anonymous versions from Jericho and Nicopolis were
added; some call this the seventh [Greek version]. They
add an eighth, that of Lucian the martyr, who emended
the earlier ones judiciously (*feliciter*), and was well liked
by the Constantinopolitans. The ninth was the Hesychian,
which was used in Egypt and Alexandria. The Greek fathers say that a tenth was made from the Latin of Jerome.

VI. A number of old Latin versions circulated at an early
date, made, however, not from the sources but from the
Greek. One popular one was called the "Itala," as Augustine
tells us (*De doctrina Christiana* 2.15). Jerome issued two
more, one from the Septuagint, the other carefully on the
basis of the true Hebrew and Greek texts. This is regarded
as the Vulgate of today, but it has been corrupted with the
passage of time in many ways, for which reason a number
of learned men, Lorenzo Valla, Faber Stapulensis, Cajetan,
Arias Montanus, and others, have made corrections. Other
translations are more recent, both into Latin and into the
vernacular and other languages. It is not necessary to speak
of them, as they are well known. From the above it can be
seen that it has been the constant practice of the church
to use translations.

VII. The inscription on the cross was not written in three
languages for sacred purposes, but because at that time
they were the languages of greatest prestige and widest

use, and so most suitable for spreading the knowledge of Christ throughout the world, which was God's purpose in that inscription.

VIII. The unity of the church is not preserved by language, but by unity of teaching (Eph. 4:3), and the first council was lawfully convened and produced good results, in spite of diversity of language.

IX. The majesty of Scripture arises from the message rather than from the words; if these three languages seem to increase its majesty, this is *per accidens* because of the prejudice (*superstitio*) of an untaught community, not from reality.

X. We do not deny that these three languages have been retained in the assemblies of the better educated, and the business of the church carried on, and controversies settled, in them, when they were no longer vernaculars; but they have not had the same value among the people, and in worship, where the faith and devotion of every person is to be supported, that he may understand in accordance with his ability.

XI. Although we do not deny that the Hebrew language was corrupted in various ways during the captivity, through contact with neighboring people, and many Chaldean and Syrian words introduced, it does not follow either that the text was corrupted in any way or that it was not understood by the people to whom it was addressed, because Zechariah, Haggai, and Malachi wrote in pure Hebrew, which they would not have done unless the people understood it. Also it can be learned from Nehemiah 8:8 that Ezra read the book of the law before all the people, to which they are said to have listened, which they could not have done if they did not understand, and if Ezra and the Levites are said to have interpreted what they read, this is to be understood as an explanation of the meaning rather than a translation of the words.

XII. Although translations are not authentic formally and with respect to the form of teaching, they ought nonetheless to be used in church, because if they are correct and in agreement with the sources, they are always authentic materially and with respect to the content of teaching.

XIII. From the above, it is clear what the authority of translations is. Although they are of great value for the instruction of believers, no other version can or should be regarded as on a par with the original, much less as superior. (1) Because no other version has any weight which the Hebrew or Greek source does not possess more fully, since in the sources not only the content (*res et sententiae*), but also the very words, were directly spoken (*dictata*) by the Holy Spirit, which cannot be said of any version. (2) Because it is one thing to be an interpreter (*interpres*), but another to be a prophet (*vates*), as Jerome says in his preface to the Pentateuch. The prophet, being inspired, cannot err, but the interpreter, being human, lacks no human quality, and so is always subject to error. (3) The translations are all streams; the original text the source whence they take their lasting quality. One is the rule, the other the ruled which has merely human authority.

XIV. But not all authority is to be taken away from the translations; here two aspects of divine authority must be rightly distinguished, that of substance and that of words. The first is concerned with the substance of doctrine, and is the internal form of Scripture; the second with the accident of writing, which is its external and accidental form. The source has both, for it is inspired both in substance and in words, but translations have only the first, because they are expressed in human, not divine, words.

XV. From this it is evident that translations as such are not authentic and canonical in themselves, because they were produced by human effort and skill, and at that point are subject to error, and may be corrected, but they are authentic with regard to the doctrine they contain, which is divine and infallible. So they do not support divine faith formally as to words, but materially as to the teaching they contain.

XVI. Perfection in substance and truth, to which nothing can be added and from which nothing can be taken away, is one thing; the perfection of a particular version is another. The first is a pure divine work, which is absolutely and in every way self-certifying; such is in the Word proclaimed in the versions. The second is a human work, and so subject to error and correction, to which great, but nevertheless human, authority can be assigned, which comes from its conformity and fidelity to the original text, and is not of divine quality.

XVII. Assurance of the conformity of translations with the original is of two kinds. The first is merely grammatical and of human knowledge, by knowing the conformity of the words of the translations to the original; this is the work of the better educated who understand the languages. But the second is spiritual and of divine faith respecting the conformity of substance and teaching, and is the concern of individual believers in accordance with the measure of Christ's gift, according to that saying of Christ, "My sheep hear my voice" (John 10:27), and this one of Paul: "The spiritual man judges all things" (I Cor. 2:15). Therefore, although the unlearned person is ignorant of the languages, he relies on the faithfulness of the translations as to the substance of the faith, to learn from the analogy of the faith and the interdependence of the dogmas: "If anyone desires to do his will, he will know of the doctrine, whether it be of God, or whether I speak on my own authority" (John 7:17).

XVIII. It is one thing to conform to the original, another to be on a par with it. Any accurate translation conforms to the original because the same teaching, in substance, is presented; but it is not for that reason on a par with it, because the form of expression is human, not divine.

xix. Although a given translation made by human beings subject to error is not to be regarded as divine and infallible verbally, it can be properly so regarded in substance if it faithfully renders the divine truth of the sources, for the word which a minister of the gospel preaches does not fail to be divine and infallible, and to uphold our faith, although proclaimed by him in human words. But faith does not depend on the authority of translators or ministers, but on the substance (*res ipsi*) which is, in truth and authenticity, in the versions.[3]

xx. If a version should contain the pure word of God in God's words (*verbis divinis*), there would be no reason to correct it, for the sources neither can nor should be corrected, as they are inspired both in content and in words, but because God's word is given to us in human words, correction is possible, not of the doctrine itself, which remains always and everywhere the same, but of the language, which can be rendered differently by different people in accordance with the measure of Christ's gift, especially in difficult and obscure passages.

3. The high regard for preaching in the Reformed ecclesiology is here illustrated—the sermon is the word of God "in very truth," as the liturgy of the Reformed Church in America says. The sermon continues the work of Bible translation; hence the importance of an educated ministry.

The Authenticity
of the Septuagint

QUESTION **14** Is the Septuagint version of the Old Testament authentic? (Negative)

I. Among the Greek versions of the Old Testament, that of the seventy-two translators rightly holds first place among us. It held this honor both among Jews and among Christians, both in the East and in the West, so that Jews in their synagogues and Christians in their churches used to read in public only from it or from versions made from it. All other translations approved by the church in ancient times, with the sole exception of the Syriac, were made from it; that is, the Arabic, Ethiopic, Armenian, Illyrian, Gothic, and the Latin before Jerome. The Greek and many Eastern churches accept it to this day, satisfied with it alone.

II. We are not concerned with such questions as the time and manner of the composition of this version: whether it was done under the auspices of Ptolemy Philadelphus and at his expense, or, as Scaliger believes (epistle 14), by Jews who were convinced of its value; whether the seventy-two in separate cells completed their work in exactly seventy-two days, and in the same harmony as if everyone, separate from the others, had begun and completed the whole work, and other stories of this kind that are told concerning these translators, whether by Aristeas, who began the detailed reporting of this work in a special pamphlet, or by Josephus and the Christians, who, because the version was in use, easily held such accounts before them, eagerly seizing any help toward establishing its authority. These are questions of history and therefore do not affect our present purpose, although, if we may speak our mind, we readily agree with those by whom all these accounts are held greatly suspect and of doubtful trustworthiness. Jerome had already, in his time, begun to expose their emptiness (*vanitas*) and to refute them, which more recent scholars have done more clearly and strongly: Vives, in his note on Augustine's *City of God* 18.42,[1] Scaliger in his commentary on Eusebius, Drusius, Casaubon, Wouverius, Ussher, Rivet, Heinsius, and others. Here we are discussing the authority [of the Septuagint]: whether such is to be attributed to it, that it be regarded as inspired and authentic.

III. Although not all Roman Catholics speak in the same way, many agree that this version was produced under divine guidance (*factum divinitus*), and rightly holds divine authority, and therefore the translators are to be regarded not as interpreters but as prophets, who, that they might not err, had the help of the Holy Spirit in a special way, as Bellarmine says (*De Verbo Dei* 2.6), with whom Baylis, Stapleton, Carthusius, and D'Espeires all agree, and so especially does John Morinus, who tries hard to establish the authenticity of this version. Among our scholars, that most learned man Isaac Voss tries to uphold the same idea, by a number of arguments, in a special treatise.

IV. We, although we do not deny that it is of great au-

---

1. Augustine, it will be remembered, accepts some of these traditions. In fact, the argument about the Septuagint, in this question, is one on which the Reformers did take a different attitude from that of many church fathers, Augustine included.

thority in the church, yet regard this authority as human, not divine, since what was done by the translators was by human effort only, not by prophets and men who were "God-breathed" by the direct inspiration of the Holy Spirit.

V. It is not, therefore, to be asked whether it should have any authority in the church. We concede that it is of great weight, and rightly to be preferred to other translations. (1) It is the oldest of all, made two thousand years ago, and so to be honored for its hoary hair.[2] (2) It was read both in public and in private by the Jews wherever they were dispersed. (3) The apostles and evangelists used it in quoting many Old Testament passages, and consecrated it, so to speak, by their writings. (4) The apostles gave it to the church, when through it they conquered the world for Christ, and so the Gentile church was born through it, and nourished by this milk. (5) The church, both Greek and Latin, used it as the common version (*pro vulgata*) for six hundred years. (6) The old fathers and ecclesiastical writers explained it in commentaries, taught it to the people in homilies, and strangled the rising heresies with it, and drew from it, in councils, canons for the direction of faith and conduct. But it must be asked whether this authority is such that it ought be regarded as authentic and on a par with the sources, which our adversaries teach and we deny.

VI. The reasons are (1) it was composed by human effort, not by inspired men; its authors were interpreters, not prophets, who lived after Malachi, who is called by the Jews the seal of the prophets.[3] This is clear from Aristeas's testimony that the translators conferred with one another, and discussed everything among themselves until they were all in agreement. But if they conferred among them-

2. See Leviticus 19:32. The honor given to the elder in society is, by analogy, extended to the eldest translation.

3. *Qui vocatur sigillum prophetarum a Judaeis*; one notes the tendency to "canonize the Jewish church."

selves, they did not prophesy, for the sacred writers never conferred with others, but put everything into writing without discussion or delay. (2) If they wrote by the breath of the Holy Spirit, their number was excessive, when one would have been enough, nor was there any need of learned men, familiar with the Hebrew and Greek tongues, if the work was done without study and without human effort. (3) In many ways it does not agree with the sources, but contains a number of discrepancies, as is shown by those who have discussed this argument, so that Morinus is forced to admit, "No more authority can be ascribed to this version than to others made by human endeavor." (4) Because it does not now exist in a pure state, but with corruption and interpolation to a great degree, we have only its debris and remnants, and today it can hardly be called the Septuagint version; it is like the ship *Argo* which was so often rebuilt that it was no longer either the same or something other, as Jerome often remarked (epistle 69, to Augustine; prefaces to Ezra and Chronicles). So today it is confidently maintained among the learned that it is from the κοινή version that may be called "Lucianic,"[4] on the authority of Jerome (epistle to Sunias and Fretellas).

VII. If the apostles often made use of this version, they did not do so because they believed that it was authentic and of divine quality, but because at that time it was most widely used and accepted, and because, where the meaning and truth are plain, they did not wish to stir up controversy or arouse scruples among the weak, but they left unchanged by a holy economy whatever, if changed, would have offended, especially when no change of meaning was involved. They did not [make changes] except where there was a reason. When the Septuagint is not only awkward, but also out of harmony with the truth, they used the sources in preference to it, as Jerome notes (*Contra Ruf-*

---

4. See question 13, paragraph 5. κοινή may be taken as "vernacular."

finan, book 2) and as can easily be seen by comparing Matthew 2:15 with Hosea 11:1; John 19:37 with Zechariah 12:10; Jeremiah 31:15 with Matthew 2:18; Isaiah 25:8 with I Corinthians 15:54, and many other passages.

VIII. The evidences (*testimonia*) which are brought forward in the New Testament from the Septuagint are authentic, not in themselves, or because they were translated by the seventy from Hebrew into Greek; but in their situation (*per accidens*) as approved and sanctified by the Holy Spirit by means of his inbreathing (*afflatus*), they were employed by the evangelists in the sacred narrative.[5]

IX. If many of the patristic writers gave high honor to this version, and asserted its authenticity, as it cannot be denied that Irenaeus, Clement of Alexandria, Augustine, and others were inclined to do, this was from feeling (*affectus*) rather than from reflection (*studium*). They were unlearned in the Hebrew language; nor were they obliged to judge the words [of the seventy], since no less than the seventy were they subject to human errors and feelings. But the more learned among them, such as Origen and Jerome, were of very different opinion, and taught that [the seventy] were translators, not prophets.

X. Although the church used this version for many years, it does not follow that it used it as authentic and of divine quality, but only that it was held in great esteem. This common usage ought not to weaken the freedom of consulting the sources when there is reason to do so.

XI. The great discrepancies in chronology which occur between the Hebrew text and the Septuagint do not suggest the authenticity of the latter but its corruption....[6]

---

5. The New Testament is inspired, but not necessarily the writings that it quotes, as has been said earlier when discussing the Apocrypha.

6. The remainder of this question, paragraphs 11 – 15, has been omitted. It consists of detailed examination of problems in Old Testament chronology. Specialists will go to the full texts of the originals.

The Authenticity
of the Vulgate

QUESTION **15** Is the Vulgate version authentic? (Negative, against the Roman Catholics)

I. It is not to be asked whether the Vulgate has value, and frequently presents the truth very effectively. No one denies this. Nor is it to be asked whether it was in past times and over a long period used in the church; this is understood by all. But it must be asked whether it is of authentic truth and to be given equal authority with the sources, and given precedence over all other translations, which we deny. The Roman Catholics affirm this on the basis of the canon of the Council of Trent, session 4, decree 1: "If anyone does not accept these books in their entirety, with all their parts, as they have customarily been read in the Catholic church, and as they are found in the old Vulgate edition, let him be anathema"; and again, "This same holy synod, knowing that no small gain will accrue for the church if, among all the Latin versions of the sacred books that are in circulation, one be recognized as authentic, understands, commands, and decrees that that old and Vulgate edition, which, by the usage of so many centuries, has been approved in the church, be held authentic for public reading, preaching, and teaching, and that no one dare or presume to reject it for any reason."

II. It is true that Roman Catholics differ as to the meaning of this canon. Some, like Bellarmine, Serarius, Salmeron, Mariana, and others, hold that it does not contrast this version with sources, but only with the other Latin translations in circulation, and they believe that it can be emended and corrected from the sources. Others say that it has been ruled absolutely authentic, so that it cannot be improved and is to be preferred to all other editions, and even the original manuscripts can be corrected from it, as if they were corrupted; such is the teaching of Cano, Valentia, Gordon, Gretserus, Suarez, and others. Anyone who studies the language of the canon will readily understand that the canon inclines toward the latter opinion. For if [the Vulgate] cannot be rejected for any reason, then it cannot be rejected because of the Hebrew text....[1]

III. However, although we hold the Vulgate in high esteem as ancient, we deny that it is authoritative. (1) Because it was produced by human effort; it does not have an inspired author, which an authoritative version requires. For whether the author was Jerome, as the Roman Catholics maintain, or some earlier person who had prepared the version called "Itala" and "Vulgate," or Sixtus V and Clement VIII, who corrected the old usage of the church at many points, none of them was inspired.

IV. (2) Neither before the decree of the council, nor later, was it authoritative. Not before, because it contained numerous errors, as many Roman Catholics—Nicholas of Lyra, P. Burgensis, Driedo, Jerome of Oleastro, Cajetan, and others, notably Isidore Clarius, who stated that he had found eight thousand errors in the Vulgate—freely admit.

---

1. Here and in paragraph 4 below I have omitted some quotations which add no new idea, and are not always readily located.

It cannot be called authoritative after the council, because the council cannot make that which was not authentic into something authentic, just as it cannot make a non-canonical book canonical, but only declare it to be such; this [privilege] belongs to God alone, who can confer divine authority on any writing that he wishes, but [a council] can only declare that a version is faithful and conforms to its source, or, if faults have crept in, it can correct them and require the use [of the corrections] in the public services of worship.

v. (3) Because in many places it differs from the sources, as Clement VIII recognized in the case of the redaction of Sixtus V. Although the Sixtine version was called authoritative by the council, and had been carefully corrected on the authority of Sixtus, yet Clement undertook its revision, restored many readings that Sixtus had rejected, and changed and corrected others, as is evident from the collection of examples by Thomas James, who besides many other variants, found about two thousand readings whose truth was confirmed against the Hebrew and Greek on the apostolic authority of Sixtus which Clement revised and corrected on the basis of the sources, by the same authority. This cannot, as Clement urges, be ascribed to the fault of the press. Who can believe that a thousand errors entered through the fault of the press, when Sixtus labored so diligently? That the Clementine edition, which, following the Sixtine, Clement declared authoritative, is full of errors, its own preface admits: "Receive, therefore, Christian reader, with the approval of that same pontiff, a Vulgate edition of the Holy Scriptures corrected with whatever care could be given; although it is difficult to call it final in every part, on account of human weakness, yet it cannot be doubted to be more corrected and purer than all the others which have been published up to now." If it is truly difficult to call it final in every part, but only purer than all that have been published up to now, it cannot be denied that correctors may appear later, nor can it be said that the council has completely corrected it. . . . Bellarmine, who was one of the editors, does not conceal this fact. He wrote to L. Brugensis, "The Vulgate Bible was not fully corrected by us; for good reasons we left much undone which seemed to call for correction."[2]

VI. (4) Many Roman Catholics—Erasmus, Valla, Pagninus, Cajetan, Jerome of Oleastro, Forerius, Sixtus Senensis—formerly recognized numerous errors in the Vulgate, and today well-known interpreters, who commonly appeal from it to the sources, do the same—Salmeron, Bonfrerius, Serarius, Masius, Muisius, and many others.

VII. (5) There are many places which have faulty rendering with grave error, in circumstance or tendency. Genesis 3:15 reads, "she will crush," as if it referred to the blessed virgin, while the source reads "it," that is, the seed. Genesis 14:18 [reads,] "he was indeed a priest," for "and he was," and Genesis 48:16 has "let my name be invoked over them," for "let my name be named among them. . . ."[3]

VIII. (6) Whatever this version is, which they hold was prepared in part from that old one that is called "Itala" by Augustine, and the Vulgate itself by Jerome, and partly from the new one of Jerome, it cannot be authoritative, for the [old] Vulgate was not inspired. If it had been, it would have been improper for Jerome to revise it. Nor can the new [Vulgate], which, by Jerome's own statement, he revised from the older, be so regarded.

IX. The Council of Trent canonized a version that was not yet in existence, but which appeared forty-six years later, for the decree was made in 1546, and in 1590 the

2. This paragraph also has been abbreviated.

3. Most of this paragraph has also been omitted. No new point is made, and a comparison of the Hebrew, Greek, and Latin texts on the basis of seventeenth-century editions is of limited value today.

work was completed and published by Sixtus V; two years later by Clement VIII. But what council could approve and declare authentic an edition which it had not seen and which in its time had not been made?

x. Although the Hebrews and Greeks have their authentic texts, it does not follow that the Latins deserve theirs, because the situation is not the same for them. It is agreed that the Hebrew text of the Old Testament and the Greek of the New came from prophets and apostles who were inspired by the Holy Spirit, but no one would say that the authors and advocates of the Vulgate were inspired in the same way.

xi. The use of a version over a long period of time can properly support its authority, but cannot give it such authenticity as would make it wrong to depart from it for any reason. Such authenticity depends on divine inspiration, not on long usage. Further, whatever was the use of this version, it was so used only in the Latin church, not in the Greek and Eastern.

xii. The true and proper cause of the authenticity of a version is not the witness of the Fathers, or the practice of the church, or the decision of a council. For Bellarmine himself points out that the church does not make books authentic, but declares them to be so (*De Verbo Dei* 1.10). So a version that is not authentic in itself cannot be declared so by the church.

xiii. It is not necessary for a person who is ignorant of Hebrew and Greek to hold the Vulgate as authoritative in order to know whether he is reading Scripture or not. For he can recognize the truth of Scripture in the vernacular versions which he reads and understands no less than in the Vulgate which he does not understand.[4]

4. An understatement of a kind quite common in Turretin, and one to which Latin idiom lends itself, in such expressions as *non semel, non pauca, non sine numine*, as well as this *non minus*.

The Perfection of Scripture

QUESTION **16**

> Does Scripture contain whatever is necessary for salvation to the extent that after it was given there was no need for unwritten traditions?[1] (Affirmative)

I. In order to avoid the tribunal of Scripture, which they know as an adversary, the Roman Catholics not only reject its authenticity and integrity, but also seek to deny its perfection and perspicuity. So the question of the perfection of Scripture stands between us and them.

II. On the nature of the question, note (1) it is not to be asked whether Scripture records everything that Christ and the saints said or did, or [whether any omitted item] has some significance for religion. We do not deny that many things were done by Christ that were not recorded in writing (John 20:30), and there are many matters, appendices and bylaws, as it were, to religion, dealing with the worship and polity of the church, which are not specifically covered by Scripture, and are left to the decision

---

1. Turretin has at last concluded his answer to the question, "What is Scripture?" It is the canonical books in Hebrew and Greek, as has been shown in questions 7 – 15. Now begins a discussion of the qualities of Scripture. Questions 7 – 15 are in large part an excursus called for by the polemics of his century; the lasting thrust of the argument proceeds from the nature of the authority of Scripture (questions 4 – 6) to the specific qualities of Scripture (questions 16 – 17) and is analogous to the presentation of the doctrine of God in locus 3, which proceeds from existence to properties.

of the rulers of the church, who should take care that all things are done properly in the church (I Cor. 14:40). The question concerns matters necessary for salvation, whether of faith or of conduct: whether all of these are in the Scripture, so that it can be a full and sufficient rule of faith and practice, which we affirm and our adversaries deny.

III. (2) The question is not whether all [doctrines] must be stated in literal terms and exact words, or directly and explicitly, in Scripture; we admit that many things are properly deduced from Scripture by logical reasoning, and then regarded as the word of God.[2] But the question is whether [all doctrines] are so stated in Scripture, either in express statements or as valid conclusions drawn from it, that there is no need for another unwritten principle of faith from which knowledge affecting religion and salvation should be sought.

IV. (3) This is not a question of intensive or qualitative perfection, which is found in the detailed truth of dogmas and precepts and a completely perfected means of communicating them. It is a question of extensive and quantitative perfection, which extends to all articles of faith and practice. The first is found partially in individual portions of Scripture; the second in the whole.

V. (4) This is not a question whether the perfection of Scripture as to degree (*gradus*) always existed. We admit that revelation changed in accordance with the different ages of the church, so that as the church grew, revelation grew, not as to the substance of the articles of faith, which were always the same, but as to the clarity of their manifestation and application. But the question is whether now

2. In locus 1 (*De theologia*) Turretin assigns a very high place to reason, and hence to philosophy, in theology. Specifically (questions 12 and 13, *De usu consequentiarum*) he argues that a legitimate conclusion drawn from a scriptural datum has the force of the word of God.

[the Scripture], without any supplement of tradition, is the sufficient rule of faith and conduct.

VI. (5) The question is not whether there ever was an oral tradition in the church. We admit that God once taught the church by an unwritten word, as before Moses. But the question is whether, once the Scripture had been committed to writing, there were oral traditions which should be received with the same reverence as Scripture, which the Roman Catholics teach and we deny.

VII. (6) It is not to be asked whether all traditions whatsoever are to be completely rejected, for we grant that there are historical traditions which record events and ritual traditions which deal with rites and ceremonies of optional nature. It is a question only of dogmatic and moral traditions, that is, ones that concern either faith or conduct. We deny that such are given except in Scripture.

VIII. (7) It is not a question whether divine and apostolic traditions, that is, all teachings which were handed down by Christ or the apostles, are to be accepted; everyone readily grants this. The question is whether any such traditions are given except in Scripture. Therefore, until our adversaries can show by an unquestionable proof that their unwritten traditions truly rest on Christ and the apostles, which will never be done, we shall reject them as human work.

IX. The question therefore comes to this: does Scripture contain perfectly, not absolutely everything, but whatever is necessary for salvation, not explicitly and in exact words, but with equal force [to explicit statement] or by valid conclusion (*aequipollenter vel per legitimam consequentiam*), so that there is no need to resort to any unwritten word; or, is Scripture a full and sufficient rule of faith and conduct, not merely a partial and inadequate one? We uphold the first; the Roman Catholics, who maintain "the unwritten traditions, whether referring to faith or to conduct (*mores*), are to be received with the same pious feeling and reverence as Scripture" (Council of Trent, session 4; Bellarmine, *De Verbo Dei* 4.2 – 3), uphold the second.

x. The Jews anticipated the Roman Catholics in accepting traditions. They divided the law into the written, and the oral, which Moses, receiving on Mount Sinai, delivered to Joshua, he to the seventy elders (Num. 11:16), they to the prophets, they to the Great Synagogue, until at last it was written and codified in the Talmud. So various "secondary traditions" (δευτερώσεις), for which Christ rebuked them, developed among them, which were a wile of Satan by which he the more easily called the Jews away from the written law. By the same device he brought it about that the Roman Catholics thought out the double law of God, written and unwritten, as if Christ and the apostles taught much by the spoken word that they never passed on in writing. Hence arose the "unwritten traditions," so called not because they were never written, but, according to Bellarmine, because they were not written by the original author, or because they are not found in any apostolic writing.

xi. In order not to seem to uphold the insufficiency of Scripture, some among them, such as Stapleton and Serarius, distinguished between explicit and implicit sufficiency, or, like Perronius, between indirect and direct. Scripture is recognized by them as insufficient in the direct and explicit sense, but it can be called sufficient in an indirect and implicit sense, because it is supplemented, in those matters for which in itself it is insufficient, by the church and tradition.

xii. We, on the other hand, attribute to Scripture a direct and explicit sufficiency and perfection, such that there is no necessity of resorting to any other tradition, even one offered as divine and apostolic.

xiii. [The reasons are:] (1) Paul says that all Scripture is inspired by God (πασᾶν γραφήν *esse* θεόπνευστον), and useful for teaching, reproof, correction, and training in righteousness, that the man of God may be complete, equipped for every good work (II Tim. 3:16 – 17). Here lie a number of arguments for the perfection of Scripture. First that the sacred writings can instruct for salvation (v. 15). Who would ask for more than that we be made capable of salvation? Second, it is useful for all purposes, theoretical and practical: for teaching faith, and for guiding conduct. Third, it can make the man of God complete for every good work. But what is enough for the shepherds (*pastores*) is enough for the sheep.[3]

XIV. The Roman Catholics make futile objections. First, [they say] to be called useful is not to be called sufficient. Water is necessary for life, air for health, but they are not enough. [We reply] what is useful, not only for some purpose, but universally, for all, by a total and adequate usefulness, not a partial and incomplete one, is sufficient of necessity. But Scripture is presented as such, when it is said to be able to instruct for salvation and to be useful for instruction in truth, refutation of error, the correction of evil and the growth of good. Nothing more is needed for perfection. Similar [objections] brought forward are no more relevant; for it is one thing to speak of usefulness that is directed toward some distant and incidental purpose, which is the function of air in health and of water in life, for such usefulness may indeed be called a support (*adminiculum*), but not a sufficient support (*sufficientia*). But it is another thing altogether to speak of a usefulness which deals with its own immediate, natural purpose; such usefulness of necessity involves sufficiency, as when fire is

3. Since II Timothy is addressed to a "clergyman," Turretin understands "man of God" in its Old Testament sense of a prophet, or one with a special call to preach, and applies what Scripture does for the pastor, by analogy, to what it does for every believer.

called useful for burning. It is plain the Scripture is called useful in this sense. Secondly [they object] that the Old Testament is meant here [in II Tim. 3:15 – 17]. If it is called sufficient for everything, then either the New Testament has been condemned as superfluous or there is no reason why something cannot be added even today to the New Testament. [We reply] (a)[4] Paul was speaking of the whole Scripture as it existed in his day, when in fact not only the Old Testament but also several parts of the New had already been written. (b) If the Old Testament was sufficient, the New is much more so. (c) If the Old Testament was sufficient in its time, the New is not superfluous for that reason; just as the ages of the church differ, so do the degrees of revelation, not that they are made more complete as to substance of teaching, but as to circumstances and a greater clarity of presentation. (d) If the New Testament is added to the Old, it does not follow that anything can still be added to the New, because the canon of Scripture is complete in every respect, not only as to the substance of articles to be believed, but also as to the form and degree of revelation that is possible in this life. Thirdly [they object] that [II Tim. 3:15 – 17] does not say "the whole," but "all Scripture," and if this is understood strictly, this perfection would be found in any individual part of Scripture, which is absurd. But the word *all* is not to be understood here as a reference to particular parts of Scripture, or to single verses, but collectively for the whole, a sense in which it is often used (Matt. 2:3; 27:45; Acts 2:36; Luke 21:32; Acts 20:24 [25]), and so it is understood by Cornelius a Lapide, Estius, and the Catechism of the Council of Trent.

XV. (2) God expressly forbids to add to, or take away from, his Word. "You shall not add to the word which I

4. I have again substituted letters for a confusing second series of numerals in the text.

command you, nor take from it" (Deut. 4:2); "Even if we, or
an angel from heaven, should preach to you a gospel other
than[5] that which we have preached, let him be anathema"
(Gal. 1:8); "if any one adds to them, God will impose upon
him the plagues written in this book, and if anyone takes
away anything, God will take away his share of the book
of life" (Rev. 22:18 – 19). It cannot be said that this refers
only to the law given orally to Moses, which was more
extensive than the written, because the written and unwritten words of Moses differed only in form; he taught
nothing by spoken word that he did not write. So he was
ordered to write the whole law, with nothing left out, for
the perpetual use of the church, and he wrote it as a
servant of believers (Exod. 24:4; Deut. 31:9, 11, 19, etc.). Thus
often by "law" is understood the book of the law (Deut.
28:58; Josh. 1:7). Nor [can it be said] that the commandment refers to wholeness of obedience, because wholeness
of obedience implies the wholeness of the law, which is
such that it is forbidden for anyone to add to it. Nor [can
it be said] that it is a matter of additions that corrupt, not
of those that complete, because no tradition is given to
complete what has been completed already, and it is not
corruption, but simple addition that is condemned; placing along with (*appositio*), not only placing against (*op-
positio*), so that Paul does not say "contrary to," but "in
addition to," or "other than what was preached"; as Theo-
phylact rightly says, "He does not say 'if anything is
preached against,' but 'even if a little is preached besides
what has been preached.' " Any addition to the content of
the faith is corrupting, because it is added to the foundation which ought to be itself only (*unicus*), and anyone

5. *Praeter* (Vulgate, *praeterquam*; Greek, παρά. See the discussion that
follows. Turretin's understanding of the verse differs from, for example, that
of the RSV; see the older translations.

who adds to the foundation shall himself be destroyed, just as a circle is destroyed if you add the smallest point, and a correct weight is not improved if you add more than is called for. The prophets and apostles who added so much to the Mosaic canon are not to be blamed, because it is necessary to distinguish the ages of the church in accordance with which it was proper for revelation to develop, not [indeed] with regard to substance of dogmas, but with regard to form and circumstances. Paul, who declared that he had preached the whole plan of God to the believers (Acts 20:20, 27), nevertheless declared also that he taught nothing except what Moses and the prophets had taught (Acts 26:22). Further, many additions that the Roman Catholics have made are not only other than the word, but also contrary to it. And indeed, as regards John, he had in mind not only his prophecy when he forbade changing it, but also, as he was the last writer of Scripture, his apocalypse closed the canon of Scripture, and he sealed it with threats[6] in the final words. Add that the argument from equality is always valid; what is said of this book [Revelation] holds true also for the others [of the Bible].

XVI. (3) The law of God is called "perfect, reviving the soul and giving wisdom to the foolish" (Ps. 19:7). But the conversion and reviving of the soul are impossible unless everything necessary for salvation is known. Nor can it be said that this text refers only to intensive, qualitative perfection, because the law is pure without any lack in particular parts, certainly not in extensive perfection with regard to quantity and fullness; because the primary meaning of the word *tamim* ["perfect," Ps. 19:7] is a perfection from which nothing is lacking, and the very nature of the case requires this, becuase it is a question of reviving

---

6. *Extremis verbis veluti diris quibusdam obsignavit; dirae* is classic Latin for evil omens, or for the Furies.

the soul and giving wisdom to the foolish, which cannot be done except by a complete sufficiency.

XVII. (4) The purpose of Scripture requires this perfection, for it was given that we might have salvation and life from it (John 20:31; I John 5:13; Rom. 15:4). How could this purpose be accomplished, unless [Scripture] were perfect, containing all that is necessary for salvation? It was given to be canon and rule of faith (*canon et regula fidei*) but a rule which is not full and sufficient is no rule; a rule is a standard from which nothing can be taken and to which nothing can be added, "an inviolable law and infallible measure, allowing no addition or substitution," as Favorinus says.[7] It was given as the testament of Christ, and if no one dares add anything to a human will (Gal. 3:15), much less can that be done to the divine one, which the lawful heirs believe, no less safely than firmly, contains fully the final desire of the testator. Finally, it is the bond of the covenant given us by God; who would say that either more [terms], or other ones should be required, either for God to promise or to be required from us?

XVIII. (5) All dogmatic traditions outside Scripture are to be rejected. "In vain do they worship me, teaching doctrines and precepts of men" (Isa. 29:13; Matt. 15:4 – 9). Nor can it be answered that Pharisaic, not apostolic, traditions are rejected. For all teachings of human origin, not given by Scripture, are rejected as a class, and it is an arbitrary assumption to suppose that the apostles gave traditions beside Scripture. So believers are summoned "to the law and testimony" (Isa. 8:20), and destruction is threatened for those who would not speak in accordance with it. By "testimony" the traditions cannot be understood, because they are often rejected by God, but either the law itself,

7. A second-century sophist, prominent in the writings of several writers who were popular in the late Renaissance.

which is often called testimony, that is, that law which is interpretatively the testimony of God, or else it refers to the other writings of the prophets, which were added to the law. Paul forbids "thinking above what has been written" (I Cor. 4:6),[8] not only in respect to conduct, lest he seem wise to himself, according to Solomon's precept (Prov. 3:7), but also in respect to doctrine, lest anyone, puffed up by the presumption of empty wisdom, proclaim strange doctrines, other than the Scriptures, in the church, as the false apostles were doing among the Corinthians.

XIX. (6) No adequate reason can be suggested for God to wish part of his word to be written and the other part passed on only by the spoken word. And he would have guided his church badly if he had entrusted part of the necessary teaching to the unreliable tradition of human kind, since there is no tradition that cannot easily be corrupted with the passage of time. Add that no rule is given for the recognition of tradition except that based on the witness and authority of the church, and this authority itself is controversial to the highest degree. Since therefore their origin is doubtful, their authority uncertain, their content confused and ambiguous, and it is impossible to have a means of recognizing them, no one fails to see that [traditions] are properly rejected by us, that we may adhere to Scripture alone as the altogether perfect rule of faith and conduct.

XX. (7) The Fathers taught this most clearly to us. Tertullian says, "I revere the fullness of Scripture," and again, "Let Hermogenes show that it is written, and if it is not written, let him fear that woe [pronounced] upon those who add anything" (*Against Hermogenes* 21 [22]), and again, in *Against Heretics*, "There is no need among us for in-

8. Turretin writes *vetet sapere* παρ᾽ ὃ γέγραπτε *praeter id quod scriptum est*. (For this Greek, see Nestle's critical apparatus.) The King James Version, unlike the RSV and NEB, gives the specific prohibition that Turretin finds here.

quiry beyond Christ or for investigation beyond the gospel; when we believe we believe this above all: that we ought not to believe anything else." Jerome says, "What does not have authority from Scripture is brought into disrepute by the very means through which it is demonstrated." Augustine declares, "In those teachings which are clearly based on Scripture are found all that concern faith and the conduct of life" (*On Christian Doctrine* 2.20)....[9]

XXI. Although everything is not written down in all details (κατὰ μέρος), as noted in John 20:30, since an isolated detail is neither a category nor knowledge, yet they are written with regard to every element (κατ᾽ εἶδος), as to the substance of necessary teaching. So it is one thing to say that many things were said and done by Christ and the apostles that are not recorded in Scripture, which we grant, and another to say that these words and deeds were different in substance from those recorded in Scripture, which we deny.

XXII. Whatever the Roman Catholics seek to have accepted besides Scripture is sometimes actually in Scripture, like the Trinity, in substance,[10] infant baptism, which Bellarmine defends from Scripture (*De baptismo* 8), the impropriety of rebaptizing, the number of sacraments, at least those numbered [in Scripture], the admission of women to the holy fellowship (Acts 2:42; I Cor. 11:5),[11] the change from the Sabbath to the Lord's Day (Rev. 1:10; I Cor. 16:2; Col. 2:16 – 17). Or they are not dogmas necessary for

9. I have not given all of Turretin's authorities at this point. Sometimes he quotes without citing the source. Sometimes his quotations vary from modern printed texts, but I have not found any in which the difference is substantial.

10. For Turretin, the doctrine of the Trinity is fundamental, and a major example of a doctrine deduced by reason from Scripture, and therefore having the force of the word of God (locus 3, *De Deo uno et trino*, question 23).

11. Acts 2:42 seems irrelevant, but appears in two editions. The Utrecht edition reads I Corinthians 11:28, which must be an error. Acts 1:14 may have been meant.

salvation, like the perpetual virginity of Mary,[12] or they are false and imagined, like the local descent of Christ into hell, purgatory, the mass, or the return of Enoch and Elijah.[13]

XXIII. The "deposit"[14] mentioned in I Timothy 6:20 means anything but an oral, unwritten tradition: either a sounder form of the words to which he is directed (II Tim. 1:13), in opposition to profane innovations and the attacks of "wisdom falsely called," or the wealth (*talentum*) of gifts given him, which has nothing in common with a mishmash of unwritten traditions.

XXIV. Those many things which the disciples of Christ could not bear (John 16:12) do not imply the insufficiency of Scripture or the need for traditions, both because they were not new dogmas different from those given earlier (John 14:26), but the same ones spoken more clearly and demonstrated more firmly by the Spirit; and because, when later taught by the outpouring of the Spirit, they committed them to writing.

XXV. The apostle's word in II Thessalonians 2:15 does not prove that unwritten traditions were given, but indicates the twofold manner in which the same teaching was passed on; first by the spoken word, then by the written,

12. In locus 13, *De persona et statu Christi*, question 11, paragraph 21, Turretin states that Mary's perpetual virginity is "probable" and is devoutly believed for the sake of the consensus of the "old" (patristic) church. But he rejects any suggestion that she took vows (26). This attitude is in harmony with that of Zwingli. See also J. Wollebius in Beardslee, *Reformed Dogmatics* (Grand Rapids: Baker, 1977), p. 95. The emphasis in all Reformed theologians who teach this way includes an insistence that the case is not proved.

13. The return of Enoch and Elijah was an important part of popular medieval eschatology. The local descent of Christ into hell was a question on which Reformed theologians differed from both Lutherans and Roman Catholics. The Reformed doctrine, as upheld by Turretin, did not preclude the more general conclusion that the resurrection body of Christ moved in space, nor did it deny that hell was a place.

14. See Vulgate text, or Greek.

and the disjunctive particle εἴτε ("or"), which can also be copulative, as in Romans 14:8, I Corinthians 15:11, and Colossians 1:20,[15] shows diversity not in content, but in form, which could be two forms of the same thing (*alius et alius*), especially in those early times when the canon of the New Testament Scriptures had not yet been written. Finally, although not all [necessary teachings] are found in the letter which Paul wrote to the Thessalonians, it does not follow that they are not found elsewhere in Scripture.

XXVI. Tradition sometimes means any teaching which is handed down to us, whether by written or by spoken word, and sometimes a teaching handed down only by the spoken unwritten word. There is no question about tradition in the first sense, so that all dogmas contained in Scripture may be called traditions, as Paul speaks of the institution of the Eucharist (I Cor. 11:23); but we are concerned over the second.

XXVII. Direct and indirect sufficiency are distinguished, to no avail, by Perronius. [His grounds are] that it leads us to the church, which then makes good the insufficiency (*defectus*) of Scripture. [He gives these arguments:] (1) the true insufficiency of Scripture is known in this process, because if it leads us to the church which has this sufficiency, it states that in itself it does not have it. (2) In the same way the law can be said to be complete for [purposes of] salvation, for it leads to Christ in whom is salvation. (3) Scripture does not lead us to a church that sets forth new articles of faith, but [leads] in order that [the church] may interpret and apply those which are in Scripture. The reply should not be that we teach this indirect sufficiency when we hold that Scripture contains all [doctrines] necessary for salvation, if not expressly at least by logical deduc-

15. In Latin, all these verses have a *sive ... sive*, which can be read "both ... and" as well as "either ... or." In Greek, the two have the εἴτε of Turretin's text; Romans 14:8 has ἐάν ... ἐάν.

tion (*per consequentiam*), because when Scripture teaches anything in that way, it does not lead to another who teaches, but brings forth from within itself (*ex sinu suo*) [teachings] that were implicitly lying there. Nor can a similar [illustration] which is brought forward by Perronius, that of letters of credence, which do not contain everything that the envoy has in his instructions, be used here, for Scripture is not like a letter of credence, but like an edict by a ruler, which contains everything that is to be believed or done, to such extent that nothing can be added to it or taken away from it.

XXVIII. The perfection of Scripture which is affirmed by us does not exclude either the ministry (*ministerium*) of the church, which was established by God for the proclamation and application of the word, or the necessary work (*virtus*) of the Holy Spirit for internal conversion,[16] but it does exclude the need for any other rule (*regula*) for external guidance which can be added to Scripture for its completion. The plan (*regula*) that requires the hand of the builder for its completion is not for that reason imperfect.

XXIX. Positive and affirmative teachings which explain clearly (*positive*) what we must believe are one thing; negative ones which teach what is to be rejected are another. The question of the sufficiency of Scripture should not be raised concerning negative articles, as if it ought to contain the rejection of every error and heresy which had then arisen or which would arise up to our time, for just as a straight line shows its own direction and that of a line that crosses it, errors are easily refuted from the position of

16. The work of the Holy Spirit through Scripture was mentioned at the beginning of the locus, and is also discussed by Turretin in two *Disputationes de Sacrae Scripturae authoritate* (*Opera*, vol. 4). See the introduction to this volume.

truth. Our question is above all of affirmative articles, which are the very food of the soul.

xxx. "Tradition" is used both formally, for the act of passing on, and materially, for the content passed on; here we are not concerned with tradition in the first sense; we admit it in that sense for we have Scripture for that, but we are concerned with the second, in that we reject it.

xxxi. The Old Testament Scripture was perfect essentially and absolutely, because it contained the substance of doctrine necessary for salvation in the conditions of that time; but it can be called imperfect accidentally and comparatively with respect to the New Testament in regard to form of manifestation, although it is the age of manhood with regard to the Jewish church (Gal. 4).[17]

xxxii. That Jesus the son of Mary is the true Messiah, or the Son of God in the flesh, is not a new article of faith, but an explanation and application of old ones, [an explanation] which teaches in hypothesis what in the Old Testament was taught in thesis concerning the Messiah. So when Christ adds a countersignature to the bond, fulfillment to the prediction, body to the shadow, he does not offer a new teaching, but explains and illustrates an old one.[18]

xxxiii. A tradition concerning Scripture does not indicate that traditions besides Scripture were given, because the question properly is not one of beginnings (*principii*), but of preeminences (*principiatus*); whether given the Scripture we have, there is need for any unwritten tradi-

17. The sentence is difficult, both in grammar and in theology, but is a comparison of the relationship of the Old Testament first to the New and then to the Jewish church.

18. Although Turretin emphasizes that the whole message of Scripture need not be found in every part, he also holds that the perfection of the whole implies the perfection of parts. The Old Testament, as part of the perfect Scripture, must contain teaching about Jesus.

tions to make good its lacks in matters necessary for salvation. Further, tradition is formal and active, which we grant, because the oracles of God have been entrusted to the church as herald and guardian of them; but it is not material and passive, teaching some doctrine passed on apart from Scripture; this we deny. So we have Scripture through tradition, not that tradition is the beginning of belief, but that it is the means and instrument by which it comes to our hands.

XXXIV. Scripture is called perfect, not always sufficiently with regard to the object, as if it explained perfectly all the mysteries which it passes on; there are many which in themselves cannot be expressed, like God or the Trinity, but sufficiently for its purpose, because it sets forth [the mysteries] in such a way that they can be understood by us sufficiently for salvation.

XXXV. When we say that Scripture is perfect in the essence (*esse*) of the rule, we understand the whole of Scripture collectively, not the whole of Scripture in a distributive sense, that is, its individual parts, and so not in the sense that whatever is of the rule, the same is the rule.

XXXVI. Although the Fathers often spoke of traditions, these are not the unwritten ones, because they speak in different ways concerning these traditions.. Sometimes they mean by tradition that act of passing on, by which the sacred books were preserved in an unbroken succession by the church and passed on to future generations; which is the formal tradition, in which sense Origen says that he was taught by tradition that the four Gospels are unquestioned in the universal church. Secondly, ["tradition"] is often used for the written teaching, which first was presented by the spoken word, then written; thus Cyprian says, "If it is proclaimed in the gospel, or found in the letters or acts of the apostles, the sacred tradition is to be kept" (epistle 74, to Pompeius). Thirdly, ["tradition"] means teaching which is not found in Scripture in specific words, but is deduced by legitimate and necessary consequences, against those who demanded express words of Scripture, and were unwilling to accept the homoousion, because it was not a scriptural word. Thus Basil denies that the exact profession of faith by which we believe in the Father, the Son, and Holy Spirit can be obtained from Scripture, [but only] by understanding the creed, whose articles are, however, in Scripture so far as meaning is concerned (*On the Holy Spirit* 27). Fourthly, ["tradition"] means the teaching on rites and ceremonies known as the ritual tradition. Fifthly, the judgment of the teachers of the old church in the interpretation of some passage of Scripture, which they held to, not without humble veneration of antiquity, as received from the elders, because it agreed with Scripture. This can be called "tradition of meaning" or "exegetical tradition." Irenaeus often speaks of it (*Against Heresies* 3.3), and Tertullian does so often in *Concerning the Prescription of Heretics* (book 1). Sixthly, they used the word "tradition" *ad hominem*, in disputing against heretics who employed [traditions], not because they proved that which was not to be found in Scripture, but because the heretics with whom they were disputing did not recognize the Scripture, since, as Irenaeus said, "When they knew themselves defeated by the Scriptures, they turned into enemies of the Scriptures." [The Fathers] therefore disputed from the consensus of tradition and Scripture, as today we also debate with our adversaries on the basis of the Fathers, but they did not do this from the conviction that they received dogmatic traditions outside of Scripture, on the witness of Jerome: "The sword of the Lord strikes down those who, on their own accord, make charges and fabrications without the authority and witness of Scripture, as if by apostolic tradition" (*On Haggai 1*).

The Perspicuity
of Scripture

QUESTION **17**

Is Scripture so understandable in matters necessary for salvation that it can be read by a believer without external unwritten traditions or the help of the authority of the church? (Affirmative, against the Roman Catholics)

I. It is not enough for the Roman Catholics to argue the imperfection of Scripture to support the need for tradition, but, in order to keep the people from reading it, and to hide the light under a basket, the more easily to reign in the darkness, they have begun to argue for its obscurity, as if there can be no trustworthy knowledge of its meaning without the decision of the church.

II. On the nature of the question, note (1) it is not a question of the perspicuity or obscurity of the subject, or of persons; no one denies that Scripture is obscure to unbelievers and unregenerate people, to whom the gospel is its own concealment, as Paul says (II Cor. 4), and we acknowledge that the illumination of the Spirit is needed by believers for its understanding. But the question is of the obscurity or perspicuity of the object, or Scripture; is it so obscure that a believing person cannot comprehend it for salvation without the authority and decision of the church? This we deny.

III. There is no question of the obscurity of the content or mysteries taught in Scripture; both parties recognize that many mysteries taught in Scripture are so sublime that they are to the highest degree beyond our understanding, and so can be called obscure in themselves. The question concerns the manner in which these most abstruse matters are presented, and we hold that they are so moderated by the wonderful condescension (συγκατάβασις) of God that a believer who has enlightened eyes of the mind can comprehend these mysteries sufficiently for salvation if he reads carefully.

IV. It is not a question of whether the Holy Scripture is clear in all its parts, so that it guides with no interpreter and no exposition of doubtful matters, [a teaching] which Bellarmine, falsely and with calumny, charges upon us, stating it thus: "Are the Scriptures very plain and obvious so that no interpretation is needed?" (*De Verbo Dei* 3.1). On the contrary, we hold that Scripture has its own secrets, which we cannot discover, and which God wills to be in Scripture to awaken the zeal of the faithful, to increase their effort, to control human pride, and to purge the contempt that easily could have arisen from too much ease [of understanding]. But the question deals only with matters necessary for salvation, and with them only in reference to aspects which must be known; for example, the mystery of the Trinity is presented clearly as to the "what," which is necessary, but not as to the "how," which is not revealed to us, and not needed for salvation.[1] So it seemed good to God in Scripture, just as in nature, that all matters of necessity should be found almost everywhere, and could be found out easily, but that many less necessary matters be more securely hidden, so that they could not be discovered without earnest effort. Thus in addition to the

---

1. Turretin here uses the Greek words τὸ ὅτι and τὸ πῶς, although purely Latin scholastic terminology seems available. He may have preferred Greek to emphasize his distance from Rome, or it may be a leftover from the Renaissance joy at knowing Greek.

necessary food, he might have, as it were, his luxuries, his gems, and gold deeply buried, to be brought forth by unwearied labor. And just as the heavens are dotted with many stars, some greater and some less, so Scripture does not shine everywhere with equal brightness, but is variegated with clearer and more obscure passages like stars of greater or less magnitude.

v. It is not a question of whether matters necessary for salvation are presented clearly everywhere in Scripture. Indeed we grant that there are many passages that are difficult to understand, by which God wills to exercise our effort and the skill of the scholar. The question is whether [these necessary matters] are presented somewhere in such a manner that a believer can recognize their truth when he has given them serious consideration, because nothing is learned from the more obscure passages that is not found most plainly taught elsewhere. As Augustine says, "The Holy Spirit has arranged the Scriptures in such a wonderful and wholesome manner, that hunger is remedied by the plainer passages and pride by the more obscure" (*Concerning Christian Doctrine* 2.6 [7 *ad fin.*]),[2] and, "We feed on the clear passages, and are disciplined by the obscure; in the one [our] appetite is overcome, in the other [our] pride."

vi. It is not a question of a perspicuity that excludes necessary means for interpretation, such as the inner light of the Spirit, the attention of the mind, the voice and ministry of the church, lectures and commentaries, prayers and vigils. We acknowledge such means are not only useful but also normally are necessary, but we want to deny any obscurity that keeps the common people from reading Scripture, as if it were harmful or dangerous, or that leads

2. My rendering of the Latin resembles that in *The Fathers of the Church* rather than the older English version in the *Nicene and Post-Nicene Fathers*.

to a falling back on traditions when one should have taken a stand on Scripture alone.

VII. The question therefore comes to this: is Scripture so understandable in matters necessary for salvation, not with regard to what is taught but with regard to the manner of teaching, not with regard to the subject [persons], but to the object [Scripture itself], that it can be read and understood for salvation (*salutariter*) by believers without the help of external traditions? The Roman Catholics deny this; we affirm it.

VIII. That Scripture has this perspicuity is plain (1) from Scripture itself, which proclaims its lucidity. "The testimony of Jehovah is sure, enlightening the eyes" (Ps. 19:8). "Thy words are a lamp to my feet" (Ps. 119:105). "A light shining in the darkness" (II Peter 1:19). "The law is a lamp" (Prov. 6:23). The first objection of Bellarmine, who applies this to the precepts of the Law, not to the entire Scripture, has no weight. For the whole Word of God is often designated by the word *law*, and its effects, consolation and renewal, teach that it should be so understood. The glosses, [Nicholas of] Lyra, and Arias Montanus support our position.[3] Peter certainly calls the whole Word of God a lamp. [Bellarmine's] other objection, that even if "law" refers to the whole Scripture, it is not to be understood in any other sense than "because it throws light upon the matters that are understood," is no better. For Scripture is called "clear" (*lucidus*) not only because it throws light upon the matters that are understood, but also because it is clear in itself and has been made suitable for throwing light on these matters, if used by people with the eyes of faith, so that it is lucid both formally and effectively, since it throws out rays like the sun, and offers itself for the contemplation of

3. Again Turretin goes to the testimony of Roman Catholics against the decision of Trent, a Roman Catholic tradition older than that of Bellarmine, and, for him, superior.

the eye [of faith]. Finally, nothing more stupid can be said; it is as if I should say that Scripture does not enlighten unless it enlightens, for it enlightens by the very thing by which it is understood.

IX. Deuteronomy 30:11, where the word is said to be not hidden nor far away from us, refers not only to the ease of carrying out the commandments, but also to the ease of understanding without which they could never be carried out, nor does it refer to precepts alone, but to the word of God in general, so that in Romans 10:6 Paul attaches faith to this word, because [the word] is not to be implemented by works but believed by faith.

X. The gospel is said to be hidden only from unbelievers, and plain (*perspicuus*) to believers (II Cor. 4:3), not only as preached, but also as written, both because the apostles did not preach one thing and write another, and also because here the clariy (*claritas*) of the gospel is opposed to the obscurity of the Old Testament, in reading which the Jews were busied, as Paul explains in II Corinthians 3:14.

XI. (2) The following [externals] of Scripture prove its perspicuity: (a) its cause (*efficiens*), God "the Father of lights" (James 1:17), who cannot be said either to be ignorant or not to wish to speak clearly, unless his supreme goodness and wisdom are called into question; (b) its purpose, which is to serve as canon and rule of faith and morals, which would be impossible if it were not understandable (*perspicuus*); (c) its content (*materia*), namely the Law and the gospel, which are to be understood easily by everyone; (d) its form, for it is to us as a will, a treaty of alliance, the edict of a ruler, all of which must be clear and not obscure.

XII. The Fathers often recognized this, although they did not deny that the Scriptures had their profundities, which ought to stimulate the researches of the faithful. Chrysostom says that Scripture is so put together that "even the simple-minded (*idiotae*) can understand it, if only they read it carefully," and "everything there is plain and straightforward, and everything necessary is clear" (Homily 3: Concerning Lazarus). Augustine says, "In those matters which are taught (*traditia*) clearly in Scripture is found everything that leads to faith and right living" (*Concerning Christian Doctrine* 2.6, 9). Irenaeus says that the prophetic and evangelical writings are clear and without ambiguity (2.46). Gregory, in his preface to Job, declares, "Scripture contains in plain sight that which nourishes babes, just as in deeper teachings it contains that which holds great minds in admiration, as if it were some broad and deep river in which a lamb can walk but an elephant must swim."

XIII. It is one thing to speak of the ignorance and blindness of people; another to speak of the obscurity of Scripture. The first is often taught in Scripture. But the second is not, nor can it be inferred legitimately from the first, any more than it can inferred that the sun is hidden because it is not seen by the blind. If David and other believers prayed that their eyes be opened, that they might see the wonders of the law (Ps. 119:18, etc.), not the obscurity of Scripture but only human ignorance is to be inferred. In this connection the question is not whether one needs the light of the Holy Spirit to understand Scripture, as we maintain from our side, but whether Scripture is obscure to the believing and enlightened individual. Further it is one thing to speak of theoretical enlightenment, and another to speak of practical; one to speak of the first step and another to speak of the increments. David, properly speaking, did not pray for the first, but for the second.

XIV. When Christ is said to have opened the minds of the disciples, so that they might understand the Scriptures (Luke 24:45), this simply teaches that mankind by itself cannot grasp the Scriptures without the aid of grace, but it does not suggest the obscurity of Scripture, nor can the shadow that was in the minds of the disciples be imputed to the Scripture.

XV. It is one thing for there to be in Scripture difficult passages (δυσνόητα), whose difficulties can be mastered, but another for there to be insuperable (ἀνόητα) difficulties, which cannot be understood no matter how painstakingly they are investigated. Peter speaks of the first, not of the second kind (II Peter 3:15 [16]). Some difficulty, which we grant, is one thing; a total difficulty, which we deny, is another. It is one thing to say that the difficulties are in the language of Paul's letters, which we deny; another to say that they are in the very substance of what is taught, as Peter affirms, for the relative οἷς cannot be referred to the word *epistles*,[4] but to the teaching which is presented [in them]. Difficulties for the ignorant and unstable, who because of unbelief and ill will distort [the Scriptures] for their own destruction, which we recognize with Peter, are not the same as difficulties for believers, who are guided by the work of the Holy Spirit in humbly investigating them.

XVI. The obscurity of the whole of Scripture does not follow from the obscurity of some parts, such as the ancient prophecies and oracles, because either these prophecies are not about matters necessary for salvation, or, if there is some obscurity in them, it is clearly explained elsewhere. Thus the closed and sealed book (Dan. 12:4; Rev. 5:1) teaches that some prophecies are obscure until they are fulfilled, but it does not show that all Scripture is obscure, so that it cannot be understood by believers in matters necessary for salvation.

XVII. Although our knowledge of Scripture is obscure compared to the knowledge of glory, when we shall no longer see God darkly in a mirror, but face to face (I Cor.

4. Following Erasmus, Turretin reads οἷς; modern critical editions read αἷς.

13:14 [12]), it does not follow that it is obscure absolutely and in itself so far as this life is concerned, because (1) the clarity is such as to be sufficient for us in this life; such that with unveiled face we behold the glory of the Lord in the mirror of the gospel (II Cor. 3:18). (2) Paul speaks of a shadowy knowledge which is common to all pilgrims— "now," he says, "we see in a mirror." But who would say that Scripture was obscure to Paul? Therefore the passage refers only to the imperfection of our knowledge in this life and the difference between the revelation of grace and that of glory, not to the obscurity of Scripture.

XVIII. Although the Scriptures are to be searched (John 5:39), it does not follow that they are obscure everywhere, even in matters necessary for salvation. (1) We do not say that it is understandable to everyone, but only to the mind of one who is ready to learn and earnest in study. So there is need for inquiry, because Scripture is understandable only to the inquirer. All things become obscure very easily to those who read halfheartedly and carelessly. (2) We do not deny that there are in Scripture its secrets, which can be found out only by great effort and through investigation, but this does not prevent there being many other matters, and especially those necessary for salvation, which are easily seen by the eyes of the faithful.

XIX. Although the apostles were not able to understand adequately the resurrection and ascension of Christ (John 16:18), it does not follow that Scripture was obscure, because knowledge suited to the circumstances in which he is placed, and the teachings which are revealed, is enough for anyone. A full revelation of these matters can take place only after the resurrection.

XX. The knowledge of Scripture may be literal and theoretical, by which words are understood according to their denotation and grammatical construction, or spiritual and practical,[5] by which they are received in true faith. In Scripture there are many ideas understandable even to the natural (*animalis*) man, and it is possible for profane persons to debate learnedly about the most important articles of faith, but practical knowledge is only for believers (I Cor. 2:14 – 15; II Cor. 4:3).

XXI. Whatever may be claimed by our adversaries for the obscurity of Scripture with regard to the manner of transmission cannot show that it is so obscure in matters necessary for salvation that it cannot be the complete rule of faith and morals, but it is necessary that some infallible authority of the church be added to it, and recourse made to this alleged tribunal. For, in addition to the arguments which we will not repeat, such [obscurities] are not of the kind that cannot be solved by diligent study, or the matters which are found in those passages either are not necessary for salvation, or, if they are presented rather obscurely in one or more places, are explained more clearly elsewhere.

XXII. It is one thing to speak of the obscurity of Scripture as absolute and with respect to every age and state of the church; another to speak of comparative obscurity with respect to some particular period. We admit that the Old Testament Scripture is obscure by comparison to the New Testament and to the circumstances and time (*status et aetas*) of the Christian church. But this does not prevent it from being understandable in itself and adequate for the circumstances of the church of the Old Testament, to which it was given.

5. In spite of his emphasis on intellectual understanding, Turretin insists that the truly spiritual is more practical than theoretical. This is the nature of theology itself (locus 1, question 7). Intellect is an important element in humanity, but not the whole.

The Reading of Scripture

QUESTION **18**

Can Scripture be read with profit by all of the faithful, and ought it to be read without permission? (Affirmative, against the Roman Catholics)[1]

I. The doctrine of the Roman Catholics cannot be better understood than from the fourth regulation of the Index of Forbidden Books prepared on Tridentine authority, which reads: "Since it is evident from experience that if the Holy Bible is allowed in the vernacular, more harm than good will result, because of human presumption, let the Bible and all portions of it, in whatever vernacular language they are available, whether printed or in manuscript, be forbidden." Indeed, since this seemed too severe, Pius IV seemed to want to attach a qualification, when he gave permission for Bible reading, at the discretion of the pastor or bishop, for "those whom they considered capable of gaining increase in faith and piety, not injury, from such reading." But a later clarification by Clement VIII showed that this hope with regard to the rule was simply illusory, since he declared that no authority for granting such permission had been given bishops or anyone else, beyond what was

---

1. In spite of its brevity, the question is of crucial importance for an understanding of the significance of Turretin's whole theological effort. The sole authority, purity, perfection, and perspicuity of the Scriptures cease to be abstract matters of debate when the value and urgency of lay Bible study, which is grounded on these preceding questions, is the issue. See the introduction to this volume.

previously granted by the rules of the Inquisition, to whose requirements obedience must be given in this matter. So, since one hand has taken away what the other seemed to have given, they have shown that their intention is nothing less than to hide this light under a basket and take the Scriptures away from the people, so that their errors will not be exposed. We recognize that to some Roman Catholics, who think the reading of Scripture should be permitted the people, this seems a harsh tyranny, but these are few compared to those who favor its prohibition. The opinion of the latter is accepted as that of the whole church, inasmuch as it rests upon the sacred law of the council and the authority of the pope, whom the council itself, declaring that its authority was "supreme in the universal church" (session 14, 7.3), expressly asked to "define and publish that which pertains to the censorship of books" (session 25). These [rules], therefore, cannot be seen except as the universal law of the Roman Church until they are expressly revoked, whatever may be claimed to the contrary. On the other hand, we maintain that the faithful not only may read Scripture without restriction, but also ought to do so, and we insist that no permission from pastor or bishop should be required.

II. It is not a question of whether the reading of Scripture is absolutely and simply necessary for all; for not only can young children be saved without it, but there are also many illiterates among adults who have never perused it. But the question is whether it should be permitted to every person, so that no one, even if ignorant and unlearned, should be forbidden it.

III. It is not a question whether some discretion should be observed in the reading of the books of Scripture according to the individual's capacity, as younger people have customarily been restricted from reading some books of Scripture. This is not a prohibition, but a method of teaching, and can properly be employed for the sake of greater progress and edification. But the question is whether reading [the Scripture] should be forbidden to anyone, which we deny.

IV. The reasons are (1) the commandment of God, which concerns all (*omnes et singuli*) (Deut. 6:6 – 8; 31:11 – 12; Ps. 1:2; Col. 3:16; John 5:39; Josh. 1:8; II Peter 1:19; Rev. 1:3). (2) The purpose of Scripture, which is given for the service (*utilitas*) and salvation of all, and serves all as weapons against our spiritual enemies (II Tim. 3:16; Rom. 15:4; Eph. 6:17). (3) [The fact that] Scripture is the testament of the heavenly Father; who would say that a son is forbidden to read his father's will? (4) The unchanging practice of the church, both Jewish and Christian (Deut. 17:18; Acts 8:28; 17:11; II Peter 1:19; II Tim. 3:15 – 16). On nothing were the ancient fathers so urgent with one accord as in recommending and pressing for the reading of Scripture by all. See Chrysostom's sixth homily on Matthew throughout, and his first and third homilies on Matthew, where more than once he declares that ignorance of Scripture is the cause of all evils; Augustine: *Confessions* 6.5 and sermon 35 *De tempore*; Basil on Psalm 1; Cyprian: *On the Games*; Origen's ninth homily on Leviticus and his sixth on Exodus; and Jerome's letter to Laetus.

V. Anything that, instead of being useful, is very harmful and fatal in itself cannot be permitted, but it does not follow that the same is true of something that is so only incidentally (*per accidens*) because of human weakness. If people abuse Scripture, it is not in the nature of the case but incidentally because of the perversity of those who twist it into error for their own destruction (II Peter 3:16). Furthermore, if the use should be taken away because of the abuse, Scripture would be withheld not only from the laity but also from the teachers, who have abused it much more seriously, since heresies have usually originated not among common and unlearned people, but among ecclesiastics.

VI. If errors may originate from Scripture poorly understood, it is far from truth that therefore reading should be forbidden to believers; rather they should be encouraged to examine it, so that they may avoid such errors by rightly understanding it.

VII. The freedom of reading the Scriptures does not eliminate oral instruction or pastoral guidance or any other aid needed for understanding, but it simply overcomes the tyranny of those who do not wish the darkness of their errors to be threatened by the light of the divine Word.

VIII. When Christ forbade giving to dogs that which is holy and casting pearls before swine (Matt. 7:6), he did not want to disparage the reading and use of Scripture by the believers, nor, indeed, can the children of God be described as dogs or swine. He merely meant that the symbols of divine grace are not to be given to any impure sinners who come along, nor the highest mysteries of the faith to be rashly offered to unbelievers or to those who resist plain truth with desperate obstinacy, but instruction is to be accommodated to those who show themselves to be humble and teachable.

IX. It is not enough if among Roman Catholics the reading of Scripture is permitted for some, because it ought not to be granted to some as a privilege, for it is required of all as a responsibility (*per modum officii*).[2]

2. The last clause sums up the view of the place of Scripture in life toward which the previous argument is pointing. A more logical arrangement might have put question 19 before this one, rather than in the anticlimactic position that it holds, but see the interpretation given in the introduction. The first paragraph indicated the problem of the times when this was written, but the positive teaching (paragraph 9) outlasts the circumstances and polemics of a past age.

The Meaning of Scripture

QUESTION **19**

Is there in Scripture a fourfold meaning:[1] literal, allegorical, anagogical, and tropological? (Negative, against the Roman Catholics)

I. In order that the Roman Catholics may force upon us another, visible, judge of controversies—the church and the pope—besides the Scripture and the Holy Spirit speaking in it, they invent a multiple meaning in Scripture, and from this conclude that the meaning is doubtful and ambiguous. So they distinguish between literal and mystical meaning, and further divide the mystical into three parts: allegorical, tropological, and anagogical. They call it allegorical when the sacred history is applied to doctrines of the faith, like what is said in Galatians 4:22 concerning the two covenants or Sarah and Hagar; anagogical when the words of Scripture are applied to events of future ages, like what is said in Hebrews 4:3 concerning rest; tropological when applied to conduct. All this is expressed in the familiar jingle:

> Facts the letter teaches; what you'll believe, the allegory;
> What you'll do, the moral meaning; and where you're
> bound, the anagogy.[2]

---

1. I have rendered *sensus* as "meaning," although theological and historical usage have long sanctioned the phrases "threefold sense" or "fourfold sense."

2. The "jingle," which is also quoted by the editors of the Turin (1937) edition of Aquinas, has a long history, and was not new to Turretin's readers. In the original, *moralis* occurs in place of the *tropologicus* of the prose discussion.

II. We believe that Holy Scripture has one true and authentic meaning, but this meaning can be twofold, either simple or composite. A simple and historical meaning is one which consists of the statement of one fact without any further significance either as commandment or as dogma or as history. This can be one of two kinds, either strict and grammatical or figurative.[3] The strict meaning depends on the exact words; the trope on the figurative language. A composite or mixed meaning is found in oracles containing typology, part of which [oracle] is type and part antitype. This does not constitute two meanings, but two parts of one and the same meaning intended by the Holy Spirit, who covered the mystery with literal meaning. The oracle of Exodus 12:46: "You shall not break a bone of it," cannot be grasped unless the true antitype, Christ (John 19:36), is united to the true type, the paschal lamb.

III. "Literal meaning" describes not only that which is based on the strict, not figurative, meaning of the words, by which it is distinguished from "figurative meaning," as was often done by the Fathers, but it also describes the meaning intended by the Holy Spirit and expressed either strictly or in figurative language; thus Thomas [Aquinas] defines the literal meaning as "what the Holy Spirit or author intends,"[4] and Salmeron "what the Holy Spirit, the author of Scripture, wishes primarily to say, whether by the strict meaning of the language or by tropes and metaphors" (1.7). Therefore the substance (τὸ ῥητὸν) is not always to be found in the words themselves, but also in the figures of speech; in this way indeed we uphold the substance of the sacraments, because we uphold the meaning

3. *Figuratus et tropicus; tropicus* is the word commonly employed by Turretin, here and elsewhere, for a figure of speech.
4. *Summa Theologica* 1.1.10c, quoted freely. See also 1.1.9.

intended by the Holy Spirit.[5] Such also is the meaning of the parables that the Lord told, in which the scope of his intention must always be considered, nor must the literal meaning be understood simply as what is stated in the similitude, but also as including the application. So this literal meaning is always a single meaning from which, through such similitudes, other truths can be explicated.

IV. That there is a single meaning to Scripture is evident (1) from the unity of truth, because truth is single (*unicus*) and simple (*simplex*), and for that reason does not admit of several meanings, which would make it uncertain and ambiguous; (2) from the unity of form, because there is only one essential form of any one thing, and the meaning is the form of Scripture; (3) from the perspicuity of Scripture, which makes it impossible for there to be several contradictory and diverse meanings.

V. It is not a question whether there is only one idea (*conceptus*) in the meaning of Scripture; we grant that the one meaning often yields several ideas, but they are mutually dependent, especially in the composite sense composed of type and antitype. The question is whether there are in the same pericope (*locus*) different meanings not dependent upon each other, as is the opinion of Azorius (*Institutio moralis* 1.8.2), Thomas (1.1.10), Lyra, Gretserus, Becanus, Salmeron, Bellarmine, and others.

VI. Distinguish the meaning of Scripture from its application—the meaning is single, whether simple, set forth

5. Reformed theology has been accused, since Marburg, of disregarding the plain meaning of the words of institution of the Eucharist. Turretin refers to the matter here, assuming that the reader is familiar with the question, as an illustration of the difference between the words and the intent of the writer. He discusses the sacraments in another part of the present work (locus 19).

in bare histories, precepts, or prophecies, or composite in typology; whether literally in exact words or figuratively in figures of speech. But the application can be diverse—for instruction, apologetics, or discipline—which are the theoretical and practical uses of Scripture. So the allegorical, anagogical, and tropological are not different meanings, but applications of the single literal meaning; allegory and anagogy apply to instruction, and tropology applies to discipline.

VII. Allegory [in Scripture] is either innate or inferred; either intended by the Holy Spirit or invented by humans; in the latter sense it does not deal with the meaning of Scripture, but is a consequence which is developed by human interpretation, as a form of application. In the former sense it is contained within the composite meaning as one of its parts, since there can be no doubt but that it was the intention of the Holy Spirit, and therefore of his own understanding (*de ejus mente*), that what is said in Galatians 4 [21 – 31] concerning the two wives of Abraham be applied to the two covenants, and that what is said in Hebrews 4 [1 – 11] concerning rest should be applied to heavenly rest. So when we go from the sign to the thing signified we do not introduce a new meaning but we make plain what lies under the sign, so as to have the full and complete meaning intended by the Holy Spirit.

VIII. Although the mind of God is infinite, able to comprehend many, indeed an infinite number of, ideas at once, it does not follow that the meaning of Scripture is multiplex, because conclusions concerning the Word of God must not be drawn from [the nature of] the mind of God, nor is the meaning of the utterances to be measured by the richness of the speaker, which is infinite, but from his fixed and determinate intention, in accordance with which he speaks in a manner accommodated to human capacity. When God understands anything he understands it for himself, and as he is infinite, he understands according to infinity, but when he speaks he is not speaking to himself, but to us, that is, in a manner accommodated to our capacity, which is finite, and cannot understand several meanings [at once].[6]

IX. In Ezekiel 2:10 and Revelation 5:1 a double meaning of one Scripture is not indicated by the book written both inside and outside, but rather the amount of what was written in each, in one case, the woes to be inflicted upon the Jews, and in the other, the decrees of God.

X. The difficulty of [some] texts does not suggest a multiplex intention of God, but a certain ambiguity in the words, and the weakness of our understanding. Although words can, in the abstract, mean many things, in any concrete instance they can be employed by the Holy Spirit in one of those meanings, which can be found out by examining the context (*ex antecedentium et consequentium consideratione*), and by the analogy of faith.

XI. The literal meaning is sometimes understood broadly for the entire complex meaning intended by the Holy Spirit both in type and in antitype, and thus it includes within itself the mystical meaning. At other times it is taken more strictly for the meaning that the word carries directly and in itself. In this sense it is differentiated from the mystical meaning, which is not indicated by the words, but by the

6. Note that Turretin's argument does not begin here in his usual manner, by a series of scriptural citations. It is a continuance of medieval scholastic methods, but with a different conclusion, one that had been reached by different paths during the Renaissance and Reformation. Thomas Aquinas (*Sum. Theol.* 1.1.10) had argued for the multiple-meaning theory on the basis of the nature of God's mind, following Augustine (*Confessions* 12.18 – 19). Turretin, with Reformation conclusions in his background, reasons on the other side. That theology deals with God, not in himself, but in his relations to us, is a teaching that he stressed, as against Aquinas (locus 1.5.4 and question 7).

reality signified by the words, which emerges mediately from the intention of the speaker.

XII. Although we posit a composite meaning, we do not thereby reject the single truth and certainty of Scripture, which we prove against the Roman Catholics, because the truth which is set forth in these oracles has various aspects, all of which are intended by the Holy Spirit.

XIII. Since Scripture, which contains much more than words, is very rich in meaning, it is not absurd to say that the Holy Spirit wanted to give many teachings to us in the same word, but [always] one subordinated to the other so that one is the sign and figure of the other, or that they have some connection and dependency. Thus the promise given Abraham concerning his descendants refers both to Isaac as type and to Christ as antitype (Gal. 3:16). The oracle forbidding the breaking of the bones of the lamb (Exod. 12[:46]) refers both to the paschal lamb as a figure and to Christ in mystery (John 19[:36]). The promise given David, "I will be a father to him" (II Sam. 7[:14]), refers both to Solomon and to Christ (Heb. 1[:5]). The prediction in Psalm 16[:10] that the holy one will not see corruption applies both to David, although incompletely, and to Christ, completely (Acts 2:29 – 30). There are any number of such texts in Scripture, which have various aspects (σχέσεις) which must be held together in order to have the full meaning of the oracle, and they are fulfilled not all at once, but in stages over a period of time. Thus many of the ancient oracles had three aspects: for the dispensation (*status*) of the law in the Jewish church, for the dispensation of grace in the Christian church, and for the dispensation of glory in heaven. Thus Isaiah 9:1, about the people who walked in darkness and saw a great light, has three stages of fulfillment: the liberation from Babylon, the proclamation of the gospel (Matt. 4:[14 – 16]), and the final resurrection, through which those who were living in the valley of the shadow of death will see the great light of the glory of God. Likewise in Ezekiel 37, it can be observed concerning the dry bones that the oracle had already been fulfilled when the people went out from their most bitter captivity in Babylon as from the tomb (v. 12), it is being fulfilled today in the spiritual resurrection (Eph. 5:14), and it will be perfectly fulfilled in the final resurrection (John 5:25).

XIV. The various texts which the Roman Catholics bring forward to prove a multiple meaning (Hos. 11:1 with Matt. 2:15; Ps. 2:7 with Acts 13:33; II Sam. 7:14 with Heb. 1 and 5) show that there is a composite meaning of type and antitype, which is fulfilled in stages, first in the type, then in the antitype, but they do not show that there is a multiple meaning in altogether different categories (*genera*).

XV. The mystical meaning may be either sacred or ecclesiastical. The sacred is that which the Holy Spirit sets forth through the Holy Scriptures, and which is therefore based on Scripture itself. Of this sort are John 3:13[14], concerning the bronze serpent; I Corinthians 10:1 − 4, concerning the baptism of the cloud and the sea, and the Israelites' spiritual food and drink; Galatians 4:22, concerning the allegory of Abraham's two wives; and I Peter 3:[20 −]21, concerning the ark and baptism. The ecclesiastical is that which is developed by ecclesiastical writers, either for the sake of illustration, or of embellishment, which Philo Judaeus first attempted, in two books of allegories. Many of the Fathers followed him, especially Origen, who used this form of interpretation more than any other, so that he often fell into extremes, for which reason Jerome, in his letter to Avitus and Amabilis, rightly rebuked him: "Origen thinks that the brilliance of his mind is a sacrament of the church." In the latter sense, although it can be used for illustration, [the mystical meaning] has no force for proving [doctrine], because it is a human interpretation, not divine [teaching], which can suggest probabilities but not convince (*probabiliter suadere, sed non persuadere*). But the former sense has the force of proof in the teachings of the faith, because it has the Holy Spirit as author and hence is part of his intention. Therefore what is said popularly, that theology is symbolic but not scientifically demonstrative (*argumentivus*), is true only of allegories and of parables that are of human, not divine, origin.

XVI. The mystical meaning is not found in every part of Scripture, but can be legitimately recognized only where the Holy Spirit provides the occasion and foundation for it, and this must be carefully examined, so that nothing is taught except what he intends, nor drawn out beyond his intention (*scopus*).

XVII. As in every part of Scripture there is some literal meaning, either strict or figurative, so in every part the letter has one meaning, whether simple as in the historical record, or composite as in typology, although the application may be along various lines in accordance with various theoretical and practical uses.

XVIII. For a true understanding of Scripture there is need for interpretation not only of the words which are found in the versions, but also the substance, which is called "prophecy" (*prophetia*) by Paul (Rom. 12:6) and ἐπίλυσις by Peter (II Peter 1:20). This is not to be sought in anyone's personal judgment, which is in truth that "private interpretation" which Peter excluded, but from what is taught by the Scripture itself, which is its own best and surest interpreter (Neh. 8:8; Acts 17:11). In addition, after ardent prayers to God there is need for examination of the sources, knowledge of the languages, differentiation between exact and figurative use of words, collation of texts, joining of antecedents and consequences, overcoming of preconceptions, and conforming of the interpretation to the analogy of the faith, all of which can be reduced to the three heads of analysis, comparison, and analogy. Analysis is threefold: grammatical, which deals with the strict meaning; rhetorical, which deals with figurative (*tropicus*) language; and logical, which takes account of the scope and circumstances, and the relationships among the words. Comparison matches one passage of Scripture to another (Acts 9:22), by comparing the more obscure with the more understandable, similar or parallel ones with those like them, and the dissimilar with the dissimilar. The analogy of the faith (Rom. 12:6)[7] means not only a measuring standard for the faith, or a measure given to each of the believers, but also the constant harmony or agreement of all the articles (*capita*) of faith in the most glorious words of the revealed Scripture, to which all expositions must conform, lest anything be taught contrary to the articles of faith or the commandments of the Decalogue.

XIX. There must be no rash or unnecessary departure from the strict literal sense unless the passage really conflicts with the articles of faith and the commandments of love, and figurative language is clearly found in the same passage or in a parallel one. There are very reliable criteria for figurative passages: (1) when the word, strictly understood, yields either no meaning or an absurd and impossible one, as when Christ is called the "door of the sheep" (John 10[:7]), and the "true vine" (John 15:1). (2) If it contradicts the analogy of the faith, and is contrary to some accepted dogma, either theoretical or practical. For since it is certain that the Holy Spirit always agrees with himself, it cannot be supposed that any meaning that overthrew other truths taught by him originated with him. For this reason we conclude that the eucharistic words are figurative, because their strictly literal sense conflicts with various articles of faith concerning the truth of the body of

7. Greek, κατὰ τὴν ἀναλογίαν τῆς πίστεως.

Christ, his ascension into heaven, and his return in judgment. And Hosea 1:2 must be interpreted symbolically and allegorically, not literally, because a shameful act forbidden by the law, marriage with an adulteress, is commanded, in which connection Augustine's words are relevant: "If the passage forbids a shameful or evil act or requires one that is constructive or helpful, it is not figurative; if, however, it seems to require a shameful or evil act, or to forbid one that is constructive or helpful, then it is figurative (*Concerning Christian Doctrine* 3.16). The reason is that it is of God's nature to require good deeds, because he is good, and to forbid evil ones most sternly, because he is holy, although often does he permit them.[8]

XX. The means upon which our adversaries rely, beyond this rule of faith, such as the practice of the church, the consensus of the Fathers, and the decisions of councils, are, besides being all brought together in the decision of an individual pope, uncertain and based upon no foundation, and indeed are impossible and contradictory, and distract the mind with innumerable problems, rather than helping it, as we shall show in what follows.

8. Turretin has set forth his criteria for recognizing the "meaning intended by the Holy Spirit" in difficult passages of Scripture. It is to be noted that figurative meanings are to be recognized by their own nature in the context of Scripture, not by any explicit declaration of Scripture. The critical study of the Bible is required by this theology. At the same time, whatever traditions are rejected, the "rule of faith" stands as a "known" summary of biblical teaching. The limits of reason are therefore set, in theory.

The Supreme Judge of Controversies and the Interpreter of Scripture

QUESTION **20**

> Is Scripture, or God speaking in Scripture, the supreme and infallible judge of controversies and the interpreter of Scripture, rather than the church or the Roman pontifex? (Affirmative, against the Roman Catholics)

I. This question is the first and almost only one on whose account all the other controversies concerning Scripture which are discussed have been begun, for the Roman Catholics do not call the authority of Scripture into doubt, or assail its integrity and purity, or deny its perspicuity and perfection for any other reason than to be able to show that it cannot be the judge of controversies, and that it is necessary to resort to the tribunal of the church.

II. Concerning the question at issue it must be noted (1) it is not a question of every kind of decision making [in theology]—whether in every controversy of the faith a decision must be given by the church or its authorities—the orthodox[1] refute this by making such decisions themselves. The question deals only with the ultimate and infallible decision on which it is necessary to stand or fall—whether this lies within Scripture itself as we teach, or with some human being, or assembly made up of human beings, as the Roman Catholics do.

---

1. Turretin rarely uses the word *Reformed*; he usually refers to Reformed theologians as *orthodoxi*, often simply as *nos* ("we").

III. Three types of judge must be carefully distinguished. The first is the ultimate and authoritative (*supremus et* αὐτοκρατορικός) who decides authoritatively and absolutely, as supreme ruler, and from whom there is no appeal. The second is that of a functionary or minister, who gives a decision as a public official. The third is personal or private—the individual's decision regarding either the law or its interpretation. In the first case, the decision is final and absolute. In the second, it is official, but subordinate and limited by the law. In the third case, it is a personal opinion without official standing. Here we are not discussing personal or ministerial decision, but that which is supreme and infallible.

IV. (2) The question is not whether Scripture is rule and norm in controversy—on that we do not differ from the Roman Catholics; at least they want to seem to hold this, although, by teaching its obscurity and imperfection, they take away with one hand what the other gives.

V. The teachings of the Roman Catholics may be summarized thus: (1) they distinguish the norm and the judge who must make a decision on the basis of Scripture. They do indeed recognize Scripture as norm, but a partial and inadequate one to which unwritten tradition must be added; [a norm] that is not enough for settling controversies unless the decision[2] of some visible and infallible judge, who decides without ambiguity which side has the better case, supplements it, since otherwise there would be no end to disagreements. [2] But such a judge can be found nowhere except in the church, where they set up four tribunals from which there is no appeal: (1) the church, (2) the councils, (3) the Fathers, (4) the pope; but finally

2. *Sententia.* Turretin here seems to use this word as a synonym for *judicium*, which he has employed elsewhere.

when all is said the pope, to whom this supreme and infallible decision should be granted, stands alone.

VI. The following show that this is their teaching: (1) Andradius, who attended the Council of Trent, wrote, "We do not regard the right (*authoritas*) of interpreting Scripture as residing in any individual bishop, but only in the Roman pontiff, who is the head of the church, or in his authority (*imperium*), in which all her rulers (*praesules*) are united in one." (2) Bellarmine: "This judge cannot be Scripture, but the ecclesiastical prince (*princeps*), either alone or with the advice and consent of [his] fellow bishops" (*De Verbo Dei* 19). (3) Gregory of Valentia: "The Roman pontiff, who is eminent in the church for the settling of all controversies whatsoever concerning the faith, is the one in whom this authority lies" (7). This is not, however, the teaching of all [Roman Catholics], for although those who regard the pope as superior to a council ascribe this judicial authority to him, those who want a council to be superior to the pope teach otherwise, and finally there are those whose teaching is a combination of the two [doctrines], who hold that this infallible judge is the pope in council, or a council approved by the pope.

VII. We do not deny that there can be in the church a ministerial and secondary judge, who can officially moderate controversies over the faith by the Word of God, but we hold that the Holy Spirit, as its source, teaches us the true interpretation of Scripture where inner assurance is concerned. We deny that any supreme and infallible judge except Scripture need be sought with regard to external proof of the object, much less that the pope, who assumes such a task, is to be accepted. We believe that Scripture alone, or God speaking in it, is enough.

VIII. The reasons are (1) God, in both Old and New Testaments, calls us to this judge finally and without any condition. "Do according to the law which shall teach you"

(Deut. 17:10[11]); "To the teaching and the testimony" (Isa. 8:20); "They have Moses and the prophets, let them hear them" (Luke 16:29). Christ does not say, "they have priests and scribes who cannot err, let them hear them," but, "they have Moses and the prophets," that is, they have them through their writings. Thus he declares that these writings are fully sufficient for instruction, and that their authority must be accepted. In Matthew 19:28 Christ's thought is the same when he promises the apostles that after his departure they "will sit on twelve thrones judging the twelve tribes of Israel," which cannot refer to anything except judicial power that they will hold in the church through the Word. So in Matthew 22:29 Christ says to the Sadducees, "You err, not knowing the Scriptures." And elsewhere he urges the Jews to read the Scriptures (John 5:39).

IX. (2) The practice of Christ and the apostles, who appealed to the Scriptures in controversies over the faith (Matt. 4 and 22; John 5 and 10; Acts 17 — 18, and 26) and who said that they taught nothing except Moses and the prophets (Luke 24:44; Acts 26:22). Peter, by a heavenly vision, describes the Word as "word made more sure" (II Peter 1:19). The people of Berea are praised for testing teaching by the norm of Scripture, not for consulting some infallible oracle (Acts 17:11). But both Pharisees and Sadducees are rebuked for departing from it (Matt. 15:3; 22:29).

X. (3) A supreme and infallible judge is indeed one who is never wrong in his decisions, and cannot err, who is not influenced by any interested party, and from whom there can be no appeal. But all these qualities can be attributed neither to the church nor to the councils nor to the pope, for they both can err and often have done so most grievously, and they are parties to the case, standing accused as falsifiers and corruptors of Scripture, and appeal from them to Scripture is often called for (I John 4:1; Isa. 8:20; John 5:39; Acts 17:11). Only God speaking in Scripture lays claim to all these qualities in his own person, for he cannot fall into error, since he is truth itself, nor show partiality, since he is no respecter of persons, nor can there be any appeal from him, since he has no superior (*nullam agnoscit superiorem*).

XI. (4) A human being cannot be an infallible interpreter of Scripture and judge of controversies, because he is subject to error, and our faith cannot be made dependent (*resolvitur*) upon him, but only upon God on whom the meaning and teaching of Scripture depend, and who is the best interpreter of his own words, who can best make clear the meaning of the law as the only teacher (Matt. 23:8, 10), our lawgiver, who can save or destroy (James 4:12). Nor do the rulers of the church cease to be human beings, and therefore fallible, just because they are guided by the Holy Spirit, because their inspiration is merely ordinary and general, not the extraordinary and special [inspiration] which confers the gift of infallibility, such as was given the prophets and apostles.

XII. (5) If there is such a judge as the Roman Catholics claim, it is strange (1) that the Lord never mentioned the need for such an interpreter, (2) that Paul in his letters, especially in that to the Romans, never by one little word informed them of this privilege, (3) that Peter, in his catholic Epistles, did not assume this power for continuing the succession, much less exercise it himself. (4) The popes themselves have not been able, and have not wanted, to settle, by this infallible authority, many most serious controversies that have taken place within the Roman Church, between Thomists and Scotists, Dominicans and Jesuits, Jesuits and Jansenists. Why have they not overcome quarrels, and solved troublesome problems, by their infallibility? If they could, why did they not free the church from such scandals?

XIII. (6) The church cannot be made judge of controver-

sies because it would be a judge of its own case. The chief
controversy concerns the power and infallibility of the
church: on the question whether the church should decide whether the Roman Church cannot err, will the same
church sit as judge and must it be believed because it
declares itself [inerrant]? Indeed, is it to be endured that
the Holy Scripture, which all acknowledge as the infallible
Word of God, be unacceptable as judge? And that the
church, or the pope, who not only is subject to error, but
also often has erred, sit as judge of his own case, and be
infallible judge of his own infallibility, which is so uncertain? Indeed, the Roman Catholics themselves have been
forced to grant that many popes have been heretics, or
given to impious and magical practices.

XIV. (7) The Fathers agree with us. Constantine, writing
to the Nicene fathers, after he had declared that we must
understand that knowledge of God is plainly taught in the
Gospels and the books of the apostles and prophets, adds,
"Putting away, accordingly, controversy-making struggles,
we receive the answer to the problem from the divinely
inspired word." Optatus says: "You call it lawful, we call it
unlawful; the opinions of the people swing and sway between your permission and our prohibition. No one believes you, no one us; a judge must be sought from heaven,
for no decision can be found on earth for this matter. But
for what should we rush up toward heaven, when we have
this witness in the gospel?" (*De schismate Donatistarum*
5). Augustine says: "We are brothers, why do we argue?
Our father did not die intestate, he made his will, open it,
we read, why do we dispute?" (*On Psalm 1*. 11). And again,
"This controversy calls for a judge, Christ judges, and the
apostle judges with him" (*De nuptiis* 2.33). Lactantius says
that God speaks in the holy writings as the supreme judge
of all cases, against whom there is no discussion or appeal.
Gregory of Nyssa says, "The divinely inspired writing is the

assured standard of all dogmas" (*Against Eunomius* 1). Similar statements may be found in Cyprian (*Ad Caecilium*), Chrysostom (Homily 23 on Acts), and in Augustine's *On Baptism* (2.6).

XV. (8) Just as a ruler is the interpreter of his own law, so also God is the interpreter of his own Scripture, which is the law of faith and conduct. And the privilege which is proper for other writers (*authores*), that each one is the interpreter of his own words, should not be denied to God when he speaks in Scripture.

XVI. When we say that Scripture is the judge of controversies, we mean nothing other than that it serves as the source of the divine law, and the most absolute norm of faith, by which controversies over the faith can and should be clearly and understandably settled, as in a commonwealth the bases of decisions and sentences are sought in the law. So the word *judge* is used broadly and by metonymy, a normative, not a personal judge (*judex normalis, non personalis*). So it should not be confused with the subordinate judge, who decides controversies according to the norm of the law, and who applies the substance of the law (*jus legis*) to particular cases (τὰ καθ᾽ ἕκαστα) in accordance with the philosopher's saying: "The law ought to control all things, and the magistrates the particulars" (*Politics* 4.4 [1292a ad fin.]).

XVII. It is not always necessary for the judge to be distinguished from the law, as the philosopher states (*Politics* 3.6 [1282b init.?]) that the law in a matter universally required has the standing of a judge (*in jure universali praescribendo legem habere rationem judicis*),[3] but in a specific application, a particular instance, the interpreter of the law performs the duty of judge, although in a ministerial and

---

3. Turretin, who in the paragraph above quoted Aristotle in Greek, here uses a free Latin translation. Aristotle speaks of the law as sovereign (κύριος).

subordinate capacity, in which sense we do not deny that the church is a judge, but one always bound to Scripture. As in the commonwealth the sentence of a judge is valid only when it depends on, and is in harmony with, the law, and if it contradicts the law it is of no effect and appeal can be made against it, so in the church a decision of the pastors can be accepted only to the extent that it agrees with Scripture.

XVIII. Even though Scripture does not hear both sides of disputes, nor always speak in such a manner as to acquit one party expressly and condemn the other, it does not follow that it cannot be the supreme judge and perfect norm, because these responsibilities do not belong to the supreme judge, but to the secondary (*ministerialis*) one, who is obliged to pronounce sentence according to the law, and who functions through the examination of witnesses, and arguments, and by consideration of the laws, because facts, not law, are in question. But the supreme judge is one who decides, beyond any discussion, what may or may not be done according to the universal law, and to whose decision the subordinate judges are strictly bound, nor is it ever the case that the explicit condemnation of Titius or Mavius is pronounced in the laws.[4] The case now under discussion is that appropriate for a supreme judge, because it is not of fact but of the law of faith,[5] since the question is what is to be believed or not believed, a question which judge and law may determine without hearing any litigants.

XIX. It is not necessary for the supreme judge speaking in Scripture to offer us a new word constantly because of

4. The lawbook does not name individuals who are condemned. "Titius" and "Mavius" were names used, like our "John Doe," in casuistic discussions. Here they are concrete explications of the more abstract τὰ καθ' ἔκαστα above.
5. *In causa fidei de jure non de facto.*

the rise of new heresies, provided that he, who knew the future, so revealed his truth in the Word that from it faithful servants (*ministri*) can discern catholic truth and refute all errors. Thus the Fathers refuted on solid ground the heresies of Pelagius, Arius, Macedonius, and others, even though Scripture teaches nothing explicit about them.

xx. It is not necessary to have a visible judge besides Scripture for settling controversies, because[6] (1) the end of controversies is not to be hoped for in this life: "there must be factions in order that those who are genuine may be recognized" (I Cor. 11:19). Already in the time of the apostles various corruptions which were not fully overcome appeared. (2) It is one thing to defeat an adversary in practice (*de facto*), to close his mouth so that he has no more to say, but another to defeat him in theory (*de jure*), so that he possesses that by which he can be convinced, unless contumacious. Even though Scripture, because of human obstinacy, does not always accomplish the first, it nevertheless always accomplishes the second, which is enough. (3) Just as in a well-governed civil commonwealth it is sufficient to have good laws on the basis of which particular cases may be decided by the subordinate magistrates, so it is sufficient that the infallible written Word, from which individual pastors can seek the norm for deciding particular controversies, be given in the church. (4) The visible judge has not prevented the appearance of innumerable controversies, which he has not yet settled by his infallible authority, among the Roman Catholics.

xxi. Scripture has various and ambiguous meanings, not because of the nature of what is taught or the intention of the teacher, but because of the ignorance or stubbornness of the distorter. Therefore, if this ambiguity and obscurity

6. Reading *quia*, with the Utrecht edition, not *qui*, an obvious error in that of Edinburgh.

exists, it does not invalidate the authority, but demonstrates the need for the illumination of the Spirit, and the ministry of interpreting the Scriptures.

XXII. Even though it may be a question of the true interpretation of some passage in Scripture, it is not necessary to have a visible infallible judge in addition to Scripture, for Scripture is interpreted through its own contents (*seipsam*), and although a person offers such interpretation, he is not to be regarded as the author, because he does not produce anything from himself (*nihil de suo*); he adds nothing to Scripture, but brings out (*elicit et educit*) what was all along implied by it (*in ea latebat*), since anyone who legitimately reaches any conclusion from premises does not arbitrarily invent it, but discovers it by means of accepted premises contained (*latens*) within it.

XXIII. When there is discussion concerning the judge of controversies, it is not, properly speaking, a discussion of the foundations (*de principiis*), that is, of the question which is raised concerning Scripture, which as [first] principle, is assumed here, not proven; but it is a discussion of contents (*de principiatis*), that is, of the teachings contained in Scripture, which, since the authority of Scripture has been assumed, we believe can be adequately settled; we do not, however, deny that Scripture does prove itself not only authoritatively and by means of testimony, but also rationally by means of thought.

XXIV. Scripture can no more be called silent and speechless for decision making than can the church in councils or the Fathers in their writings, which our adversaries claim to be speaking and deciding. If a father speaks in his will, and a king in edicts and commissions, why can we not say that the heavenly Father in both Testaments, and the King of Kings in the divine oracles, is speaking to us in the plainest voice? Nor can the meaning be doubtful, when the whole Scripture, or the Holy Spirit speaking in it, is said to address mankind, to accuse and to judge. The law is said to speak to those who are under the law (Rom. 3:19). "They have Moses and the prophets," says Abraham to the rich man (Luke 16:29), not indeed living and seeing, but not silent and speechless, rather speaking and to be heard. So Isaiah is said to "cry out" (Rom. 9:27). Moses accuses the Jews (John 5:45). The law judges (John 7:51). "He who does not accept my words has one who judges; the word that I have spoken will judge him on the last day" (John 12:48). In the same sense the Word of God is described as judging the thoughts (Heb. 4:12).

XXV. An earthly judge should be given coercive power in matters of civil conduct. But it is different with regard to a spiritual judge in matters of conscience, because the kingdom of God is advanced by the demonstration of spiritual truth, not by physical coercion (I Cor. 2:4). Further, not only is this no place for physical coercion, but spiritual and internal [coercion] is also not desirable, either for the pious, whom God, speaking in Scripture, draws and leads to obedience by a heart-changing and appealing force (John 6:44; II Cor. 10:4), or for the impious and unbelieving, whose consciences he torments and disturbs.

XXVI. The example of Moses and Aaron cannot be used to establish a supreme and infallible judge besides Scripture. (1) Both were subordinate, not authoritative, judges: the former an extraordinary one, the latter, ordinary.[7] They decided controversies, not by their own authority, but by the law and commandment of God; Moses as the mediator for bringing [questions] to God. (Exod. 18:19) and Aaron for answering in accordance with the law; "whatever they shall teach according to the law you shall do" (Deut. 17:11). If

7. This distinction is an important commonplace in Reformed theology at this period. Extraordinary ministers, such as prophets and apostles, and, in later crises, reformers, are part of the divine economy, although not part of the polity that is assumed for "today."

they made a ruling contrary to the law, it was not to be accepted. (2) Here it is not, strictly speaking, controversies over the faith, but over ritual concerns, decisions between one kind of bloodshed, or of leprosy, and another.[8] (3) It was not the high priest alone, but every Levitical priest whose decision was to hold if given according to the requirement of the law. If the decision was rightly made, anyone who departed from it was guilty of a capital crime, according to Jeremiah, Jesus, and the apostles (Jer. 26:12 – 13; John 9:[39?]; Acts 3:[23]; 13:[8 – 11?]). (4) No valid conclusion about the pope can be drawn from the high priest, because in the New Testament there is no high priest except Christ, of whom Aaron was a type.

XXVII. The "one shepherd" of Ecclesiastes 12:11 does not refer to the priestly type of the Old Testament but to the true priest of the New, Christ Jesus, who is the good shepherd of his people (Ezek. 34:23; John 10:11), from whom all the words of wisdom come, because men of God spoke through the action of his Spirit (II Peter 1:21), as even Roman Catholics—Tirinus, Menochius, a Lapide—point out.

XXVIII. In Haggai 2:11 and Malachi 2:7 the commandment is not that one individual priest, but an unspecified number of them, be consulted and reply to questions concerning the law, nor is the reference to their infallibility, but to their responsibility, because it is said that they have not always taught the same thing, when it is immediately added, "but you have departed from the way" (Mal. 2:8).

XXIX. "Moses' seat" (*cathedra*) (Matt. 23:2) is not a succession in the office and responsibility of Moses, or the external court of a supreme judge, to whom that supreme inherent authority now under discussion is attached, both because no Moses' seat exists, and because no such privi-

8. In Deuteronomy 17:8 the Hebrew word *nega* is rendered "leprosy" by the Vulgate, the Douay version, and Turretin.

lege was given it, but it is the proclamation of the true doctrine transmitted by Moses, as stated in the glossa ordinaria on Deuteronomy 17: "Wherever is the teaching of Moses, there is Moses' seat,"[9] and wherever the teaching of Peter goes forth, there is Peter's seat. So those who were teachers of the law that Moses had transmitted were regarded as teaching in Moses' seat, as Hilary says; therefore the Pharisees were to be heard when teaching in Moses' seat, insofar as they gave the people Moses' teaching genuinely without admixture of their own leaven.

xxx. Although Christ calls us to the voice of the church as if whoever will not listen is to be regarded as a heathen and a publican (Matt. 18:17), he does not make it an infallible judge in matters of faith because (1) he speaks, not of a question of matters of faith, but of private offenses and disruptions of fellowship, which, if they cannot be resolved privately, must be referred to the public judgment of the church, where one infallible prelate does not decide for the whole church; rather, individual pastors for their particular flocks.[10] (2) Reference is made here to the Jewish discipline, which excommunicated the contumacious; this is no more applicable to the Roman than to other particular churches within their proper boundaries. (3) If an argument from similarity is used, it is required that the church be heard when it hears Christ and speaks his word, but if it departs from Christ and speaks contrary to his word anathema is to be pronounced against it (Gal. 1:8).

xxxi. Councils sometimes sought fraternal consent, not authoritative confirmation, from popes who were not pres-

9. The punctuation follows Turretin, who thereby distinguishes between the gloss and the conclusion he draws from it.

10. In the usual Reformed theory, it is pastor and elders (session or consistory) who perform this function. Turretin, in making pastors the "representative church," followed a trend that can be observed in church history, and in seventeenth-century theology.

ent, and at other times they have sought the power (*jus*) of deposing popes, and of reviewing and abrogating their acts; they have not been able to make good what they have decreed. The Fathers and individual church members could consult with [popes], in the more troublesome concerns of the church, not as infallible judges (*judices*) to whose decisions they were bound to submit their consciences, but as honored and prudent reconcilers (*arbitri*), who, before they had been filled with the poison of pride, superstition, and tyranny, were of great value in the church, especially because of the preeminence of the city [Rome].

XXXII. Even though, in the external matter of behavior, every person, unless he is willing to be excommunicated, is bound to submit himself to the decisions of synods, and should respect such judgment for the preservation of order, peace, and orthodoxy, so that the agitations of innovators (*novatorum molimina*)[11] may be suppressed, it does not follow that this judgment is supreme and infallible, because there is always [the possibility of] appeal to the internal court of conscience, where nothing binds beyond the point where we have been convinced that it agrees with the Scriptures.[12]

XXXIII. Although we maintain that a decision of private judgment is within the rights of believers, since "the spiritual man judges all things" (I Cor. 2:15) and the apostle tells us to "prove all things" (I Thess. 5:21), we do not assert against Peter (II Peter 1:21 [20]) that the Scriptures are of private interpretation, because ἐπίλυσις here does not mean the interpretation of Scripture, but the origin of the

11. By Turretin and his circle the term *novator* ("innovator" or "modernist") was applied especially to Arminians, and, more respectfully, to their brethren of the school of Saumur, implying a departure from the old Christianity which the Reformation upheld and restored.

12. An important concession to the right of private judgment, although he still feels that agreement in doctrine is to be sought, and can be achieved.

prophetic oracles, which are said to have been written, not from the private decision and experience (*impulsus et instinctus*) of any person, as is said of those who run without being sent by God (Jer. 23:21) but [the oracles were written] at the command (*ex dictamine*) of the Holy Spirit by whom they were inspired (*acti fuerunt*). So ἐπίλυσις [interpretation] does not here apply to the responsibility of the interpreter, hearer, or reader of Scripture but to the power or impulse (*vis sive impetus*) for prophesying, or to that movement (*motus*) by which the prophet is led to write or to speak. The preceding and following verses support this understanding. In them the question is not who has the right to interpret the prophets, but by whose action and movement (*impulsus et motus*) the prophets wrote, and what our attitude toward the prophecies should be (*quo loco prophetias habere debemus*); what reverence is due them and why faith must be placed in them as unquestioned oracles of God, namely, because they were not produced by the individual act and will of persons, as if they had been discovered by anyone's personal act or will, or reasoned out by anyone's judgment (*arbitrium*), but they were spoken by the inspiration and breath (*impulsus et afflatus*) of the Holy Spirit, by whom holy men of God were moved. In this sense ἐπίλυσις describes the sending of men of God to prophesy, by which God, as it were, opens the starting gate for running, as with the runners in the stadium, who, after the barriers had been removed from the starting enclosure, went forth for the race which they then began. But if ἐπίλυσις is understood as "interpretation," as is done by many because of the force of the word itself, which does mean "expound" or "explain" (Mark 4:34; Acts 19:39), then it is denied that prophecy is of personal interpretation in the matter of first principle or origin, that is, that it comes from one's own mind; it is not denied that it is personal on the part of the subject, since "personal interpretation" is not opposed to that which is common or public, but to the external gift of the Holy Spirit.[13]

XXXIV. Some wrongly conclude, from this judgment of private discretion which is assigned to every believer, that human reason is the judge of controversies, and the interpreter of Scripture, as the Socinians teach, and as has been refuted already by us, under the use of reason in theology (locus 1, question 8), because the believer is not in this matter (*hic*) moved primarily by the light of reason, but by the word (*dictamen*) of the Spirit. And although every interpreter may examine the meaning of Scripture in accordance with natural reason, one is not permitted to oppose the word of Holy Scripture, or to reject faith in it on account of some preconceived notion, possibly of contrary meaning. Human reason, which is fallible and tricky, is more certain to depart from the truth of the matter than is Holy Scripture, which is the word of truth, and truth itself, and so reason is to be made captive to faith (II Cor. 10:5), not raised above it.

XXXV. The uncertainty of human understanding (*judicium*) cannot prevent God, speaking in Scripture, from being a fit judge of our case when it cannot be known who has the Holy Spirit or is possessed by the truth. For there is no need to know directly and *a priori* who has the Spirit, but only who is speaking in accordance with Scripture, for where thought is clarified by data from Scripture, it is easy to discover *a posteriori* who is uttering the word of the Spirit and is speaking from it. Thus the people of Berea did not ask *a priori* whether Paul, who was preaching to them, was led by the Spirit, because this is known only to God, who understands the heart, but [they asked]

13. *Adventitio spiritus sancti dono*; "external" with regard to natural reason, although internal or personal in the sense of being given to a particular person.

whether Paul was speaking in accordance with Scripture; agreement [of his message] with Scripture showed them that he was not speaking on his own, but through the Holy Spirit (Acts 17:10 – 12). We conclude with the golden words of Basil: "Therefore let the divinely inspired writing be judge for us, and the verdict of truth be without reserve for those whose teachings are found in agreement with the teachings of Scripture" (epistle 189, to Eustathius the physician [3]).[14]

14. The letter, numbered 189 in Migne's *Patrologia*, is called number 80 by Turretin. It has been ascribed also to Gregory of Nyssa.

The Authority
of the Fathers

Are the writings of the Fathers the rule of truth in the teachings of the faith and the interpretation of Scripture? (Negative, against the Roman Catholics)

I. Although it can already be adequately deduced, from the preceding question, that the Fathers cannot sit as judges in controversies over the faith, yet because the Roman Catholics are forever bringing up the matter of patristic consensus and have the habit of presenting it to us as the rule of truth, a special question is called for on this issue, which is of greatest urgency in present-day discussion.[1]

II. By "Fathers" is not to be understood the apostles, the original founders and patriarchs of the Christian church, as does Augustine in his commentary on Psalm 45, but, according to well-established contemporary usage, the teachers (*doctores*) of the ancient church, who taught and explained the doctrine of salvation both in speech and in writing. [They are called Fathers] both in respect to chronology, for they lived many years before our age, and because of their teaching, for by instilling this in their disciples they begat children in the church for God.

III. Although some would regard their period as extend-

---

1. In the 1680s.

ing to the tenth century, we do not think that it should be carried beyond the sixth, because it is certain that after the six hundredth year, when antichrist raised his head, there was a great falling away, with, by the righteous judgment of God, a growing number of errors and superstitions.[2] In the first century after the death of the apostles the chief [Fathers] were Ignatius and Polycarp, of whose writings fragments survive. In the second, Justin Martyr and Irenaeus.[3] In the third, Tertullian, Clement of Alexandria, Origen, Cyprian, Arnobius, [and] Lactantius. In the fourth, Athanasius, Eusebius of Caesarea, Hilary of Poitiers, Basil, Gregory of Nazianzus, Ambrose, Jerome, Gregory of Nyssa, Epiphanius, [and] John Chrysostom. In the fifth, Augustine, Cyril of Alexandria, Theodoret, Hilary of Arles, Prosper of Aquitaine, [and] Leo I. In the sixth, Fulgentius Afer, Gelasius, Gregory the Great, and others.

IV. Among the Roman Catholics there are three types of opinions about the Fathers. First, that of those who equate them with Scripture, according to the decision of the Glossator: "The writings of the Fathers, both as individuals and as a whole, are authoritative." A second opinion opposed to them is that of those who regard the Father's writings as purely human, and who therefore deny that they are the rule of faith. This was the conclusion of Cajetan in his preface to the books of Moses, and of the wiser (*sanior*) Roman Catholics. The third opinion is that of those who hold a middle ground, teaching that the authority of in-

2. That the papacy of Boniface III (d. 607) was a great moment in the manifestation of antichrist was a commonplace of seventeenth-century Reformed teaching, expressed by Turretin in his *Disputatio* VII. *De necessaria secessione nostra ab ecclesia Romana*, paragraph 11 (*Opera*, vol. 4, p. 176); See also J. Wollebius: *Compendium theologiae Christianae* (1626), translated by Beardslee, *Reformed Dogmatics* (Grand Rapids: Baker, 1977), p. 157.

3. The chronology is confusing. The century after the death of the apostles, and centuries after the death of Christ, are not clearly distinguished; both reckonings are used.

dividual Fathers is human and fallible but that the common and universal consensus of the Fathers is divinely inspired (*divinus*)[4] and infallible in controversies. This was the teaching of the Council of Trent, when it declared, "The traditions of the Fathers, both with regard to faith and to morals, are to be received with the same reverence of mind as the Old and New Testaments."[5] And again, it forbids anyone to presume to interpret Scripture contrary to the sense which holy mother church holds and has held or contrary to the unanimous consensus of the Fathers (session 4, canon 1). Many Roman Catholics—Stapleton, Bellarmine, Cano, Valentia, and others—are in agreement.

v. But the orthodox [Reformed], although they hold the Fathers in great esteem, and hold that they are of the greatest value for understanding the true history of the ancient church, and that our agreement with that church in the chief articles of faith is manifest, nevertheless deny that they can be called authoritative (*authenticus*) in matters of faith and the interpretation of Scripture, and that their decision is one on which we must stand or fall, but [we believe] that their authority is only ecclesiastical and human, subordinate to Scripture, and of no weight except insofar as it agrees with Scripture.

vi. It is not a question of whether the Fathers are witnesses who present the consensus of the ancient church, or the opinion of the church of the times in which they lived, but whether they are judges who can settle controversies with infallible authority. The Roman Catholics maintain the latter, we the former; if we ever argue against our adversaries on the basis of the Fathers, we use them merely as witnesses, who confirm by their stand the truth

4. The same adjective that Turretin uses to describe the Bible.

5. Turretin transposes the verbs of the decree into indirect discourse, but quotes exactly the critical phrase *pari pietas affectu* (to which the council had added *ac reverentia*).

that we believe, and proclaim the faith of the church of their time, but not as judges whose decision is to be accepted absolutely and without criticism (*examen*) and who are the standard (*mensura*) of truth in the teachings of the faith or in the interpretation of Scripture.

VII. The reasons are (1) the Fathers, either individually or collectively, were not prophets and apostles, who had the privilege of infallibility by direct (*immediatus*) calling, and were furnished with extraordinary gifts, but were men, fallible and subject to error, whose knowledge was imperfect, and who could be influenced by partisan zeal (*partium studio*) and led astray in surprising fashion (*transversum*) by emotions. The indirect (*mediatus*) calling with which they were furnished did not insure that they were beyond the danger of error; not only could they be wrong, but also it is apparent that both as single individuals and as many in agreement they were often wrong on several topics, which could easily be proved. But we have Roman Catholics agreeing with us on this, like Bellarmine, who recognizes that even the most erudite Fathers were wrong, not in an inconsequential way, on many matters (*De Verbo Dei* 3.2, 10); that they contradicted one another, and that there was none who was not faulty on something (*De Christo* 2.2). Sixtus Senensis and Salmeron say the same.

VIII. (2) The works of the Fathers are corrupt and interpolated in a number of ways. This is partly due to various pseudepigraphic writings, circulated in the name of the Fathers, which, in the judgment of scholars, are recognized as false offspring, improperly attributed to the Fathers, whether by the fantasies of flatterers, or forgery of heretics, or the greed of printers or booksellers. It is partly due to corruption and falsification which has been imposed on the genuine patristic writings, which plainly have been changed in a number of ways, whether by the faults of copyists, or by the presumption of monks, and especially the wickedness of the Jesuits, who have corrected, expurgated, and emasculated them, as learned men have long complained and our [theologians] shown by many examples, as can be seen in the works of Rivet and Daillé and others.

IX. (3) The Fathers themselves recognized that their writings were not authoritative in the sense that their bare assertion must stand in the teachings which they gave on religion. Augustine wrote to Jerome: "I admit to your charity that only to the books now called canonical have I learned to pay such respect and honor as to believe most firmly that none of their authors erred in writing. . . . When I read others, however they excel in sanctity of teaching, I do not regard a statement as true because they make it, but because they have been able to convince me, either through canonical authors or by a probable reason which does not conflict with truth. Nor do I believe that you, brother, think otherwise; moreover, I say I do not believe that you want your books to be read as are the prophets and apostles, concerning whose writings, since they are free from all error, it is not permissible to doubt" (epistle 19 [82.3]). . . .[6]

X. The Roman Catholics themselves repudiate the authority of the Fathers insofar as they recognize them as in disagreement, and they freely depart from them, so untrue is it that they accept them as judges in matters of faith. Many instances, besides the references already made to Bellarmine, Sixtus Senensis, and Salmeron, could be mentioned. Cajetan, in his preface to the Pentateuch, speaking of his commentaries on Scripture, says: "If ever a suitable new meaning of a text is found, not contradicting either Holy Scripture or the teaching of the church, even though

6. "Epistle 19" is Turretin's citation. I have omitted nearly a page of further quotations from Augustine and Jerome.

differing from the main stream of sacred teachers, I ask all readers not to scorn it hastily, but to show themselves fair judges. Such authority that we should believe them because they wrote what they did is reserved for the authors of Holy Scripture alone. 'When I read others,' says Augustine, 'however they excel in holiness and in teaching, I do not regard a statement as true because they make it' ...."[7] Baronius frequently freely rebukes and refutes the Fathers, where they teach something other than what he approves. If therefore our adversaries themselves are found disdaining and despising the Fathers, even when [the Fathers] are in agreement, whenever they are unacceptable, by what power will they require them to be heard by us as judges in controversies?

XI. The universal church can and should accept whatever all teachers offer with complete agreement according to the Word of God. But if the teaching is not from the Word, but rather is contrary to it, then it is so far from true that the church should receive it, that rather it is bound to call it anathema (Gal. 1:8).

XII. Although those Fathers who were closer to the age of the apostles ought to be more pure, it does not follow that their writings can be regarded as a norm like the apostolic ones, because the gift of infallibility is by definition unique to the apostles, and does not belong to their successors, who were not endowed with the same gift.

XIII. The unity of the church is properly maintained by unity of faith transmitted in Scripture, not by the consensus of the Fathers, which it is almost impossible to discover.

7. In quoting the same sentence in the preceding paragraph Turretin (according to the text of two editions) wrote *doctrinae sanctitate*, as reflected in the translation above. Here, in the quotation from Cajetan, he gives a Latin text similar to what the *Nicene and Post-Nicene Fathers* and *The Fathers of the Church* seem to have used. I have omitted several quotations that follow this one.

XIV. The obedience due to leaders (Heb. 13:17) is not blind and mindless, as if immediate agreement were to be given to everything said or written by them, but it should be rational, that we hear them when they speak and pass on the oracles of God that they themselves received from Christ (Matt. 28:20; I Cor. 11:23).

XV. Although we are unwilling to accept the Fathers as judges in matters of faith, we do not say that their authority amounts to nothing. They can indeed be most helpful; if not in establishing faith at least in exemplifying and confirming it, so that by this witness it may conform to the faith of the old church, and it may be seen that Roman Catholics manipulate the consensus of the Fathers rather than follow it, and the dogmas which they force upon us from the early centuries, by tradition apart from Scripture, may be unheard.

XVI. It is useless for the Roman Catholics to plead the consensus of the Fathers for the resolution of controversies and the interpretation of Scripture. (1) Because, even if available, it would form only a human and probable argument, such as could be gained from the opinions of the prudent, but not one necessarily true and beyond appeal, since the Fathers submitted themselves and their opinions to Scripture. (2) Because, if not impossible, it is at least very difficult to discover such a consensus, nor is that route, long and difficult and complicated by such a massive labyrinth, suitable for the ending of controversies. This is especially so because one can hardly know what the Fathers would have felt about our controversies, both because we have very few writings of the Fathers, especially those of the first, second, and third centuries, whose opinion is preferable to that of later ones, because closer to the age of the apostles, and because what does survive from those three centuries deals mainly with questions foreign to our controversies, and is relevant to them only accidentally and in another context, and also because the Fathers both often disagreed with one another, and often changed their minds, and understood the same article of faith differently, as they grew in the knowledge of truth with age, and as elders disclaimed what they had believed when younger.

XVII. It is not to be supposed that the Fathers are despised and insulted when we take away the supreme power of decision. It is indeed necessary to take care not to steal their proper honor, but much more not to bestow too much upon them, since more dangerous sinning has been done in the latter regard than in the former. Even if they should live again, such authority could not be assigned to them, and they would speak to us as the apostles spoke to those at Lystra who were worshiping them, "We are men of the same passions as you" (Acts 14:14 – 15). [The Fathers] often declare that they wrote not to command with authority but to profit by the exercise, that they might be read, not with the obligation of obedience, but with freedom of judgment, and they offered their works as by no means on a par with the most holy Scriptures (Augustine, *Contra Faustum* 11.5 and *Contra Cresconium* 2.31).

XVIII. From the above it can easily be seen that the Fathers neither can nor should be brought in as judges in our controversies, but only as witnesses, who offer testimony to Christian truth by their striking consensus, and show the emptiness of the dogmas which the Roman Catholics have introduced, either by silence or by solid arguments. Therefore, although their writings are to be received reverently, and can be read with profit, they can have no other authority than the ecclesiastical and human, that is, subordinate and dependent on Scripture.[8]

8. Since the consensus is human and relative, this paragraph is not inconsistent with what is said above about disagreements among the Fathers. And, by extension, what is said about the limitations on the authority of the Fathers applies equally to the authority of the Reformers, and of Turretin himself.

DATE DUE